# Discourses of the Fall

## A Study of Pascal's
### *Pensées*

*Sara E. Melzer*

UNIVERSITY OF CALIFORNIA PRESS
Berkeley    Los Angeles    London

University of California Press
Berkeley and Los Angeles, California

University of California Press, Ltd.
London, England

Copyright ©1986 by The Regents of the University of California

**Library of Congress Cataloging in Publication Data**

Melzer, Sara E.
  Discourses of the fall.

  Bibliography: p.
  1. Pascal, Blaise, 1623–1662. Pensées. 2. Catholic
Church—Doctrines. 3. Apologetics—17th century.
4. Fall of man—History of doctrines—17th century.
I. Title.
B1901.P43M45   1986        230'.2        85–24519
ISBN 0–520–05540–3   (alk. paper)


Printed in the United States of America

1 2 3 4 5 6 7 8 9

*For My Parents, Mildred and Lester Melzer*

# Contents

Acknowledgments      ix

Introduction      1

1. Seventeenth-Century Discourse:
   Sin and Signs      9

   Cartesian Rationalism and Unfallen Classical Discourse   12
      Classicism and the Eclipse of Rhetoric    14
      Vaugelas and Bouhours    16
      Arnauld, Nicole, *La Logique* of Port-Royal:
        The Struggle between Semiology and Rhetoric    18
   Jansenism (the Barcosian Faction) and
      Fallen Discourse    26
   Pascal's Theory of Figures: Rhetoric as Fall and
      as Redemption    30
      The Judeo-Christian History    30

2. The Fall from Truth into Language      41

   The Hermeneutic Circle of Language    42
   Discourses of the Second Order of the Mind    49
      The Discourse of Successiveness and Sin    50
      "The Continual Reversal of Pro and Con"    54
   Discourses of the First Order of the Body    57
      The Discourse of the Machine    58

Textual Machinations and the Manipulation
    of Desire                                                                          64
The Body of Language: The Signifier                                   68

3. Two Stories of the Fall and Desire:
   Paradise/Paradigm Lost                                               75

The Aporia of the *Pensées*                                               75
The Logic of Desire as Source of the *Pensées'* Aporia    81
The Story of the Fall and Redemption: The Perspective
    of Faith                                                                           83
The Aporia of Desire: The Subversion of the Story
    of the Fall and Redemption                                           88
The Story of the Fall from the Illusion of Truth:
    The Perspective of Uncertainty                                     94
    The Cosmological Fall: Paradigm Lost                         95
    Pascal's Demystification of the Cartesian
        Code and the "New Science"                                  100
The Aporia of the Pascalian "I"                                       105

4. Reading in/of the *Pensées*                                       109

The Pascalian Challenge to the Rationalist Model
    of Reading                                                                     110
    Saint Augustine on Reading                                       113
Reading, Representation, and the Prison of Human
    Consciousness                                                               116
Reading through the "I": Descartes—Reader of
    Saint Augustine; Pascal—Reader of Montaigne      123
Reading through the "I": The History of the *Pensées'*
    Editions/Readings                                                          128
A New Model of Reading                                                   135
Christ as Model Reader: Reading the Hidden Order
    and the Hidden Author                                                  137

Conclusion                                                                           142
Notes                                                                                    147
Bibliography                                                                         163

# Acknowledgments

Certain authors, speaking of their works, say,
"My book," "My commentary," "My history," and so on. They would do better to
say, "Our book," "Our commentary," "Our
history," etc., because there is in them usually more of other people's than their own.

—Pascal

Many elements converge to give birth to a work. Certainly "my
book" is no exception. It is linked to and informed by publications
that have preceded it. My footnotes and bibliography acknowledge
my debt to them.

As for my personal debts, I would like to express my thanks
to the National Endowment for the Humanities for its generous
support of my project in its initial stages. I am also grateful to
the University of California, Los Angeles, for a career development award and for a research grant which enabled me to employ
an extremely competent research assistant, Evelyne Berman.
Evelyne provided me with excellent translations of my French
quotations. Should there be any errors, however, the fault lies
only with myself, for I either approved Evelyne's work or made
what I viewed as appropriate changes. I would like to thank
Atiyeh Showrai who conscientiously read the proof. I am indebted
to Yvette Scalzitti and Arnaud Tripet who first introduced me to
Pascal when I was a graduate student at the University of Chicago.

Many people have read my manuscript at varying stages of its evolution. I particularly want to thank a very special person with whom I feel close kinship—my brother, Arthur Melzer. When I first read his comments, written in red and spread wildly across the pages, I thought he might be retaliating for years of sibling squabbles. But when I looked attentively at his notes, I was deeply touched by the care with which he had read my manuscript. Jules Brody, whose remarks were scribbled throughout the manuscript with color-coded pens, made numerous astute observations. Domna Stanton gave me a very sensitive reading that focused my attention on subtleties I had overlooked. Anthony Pugh graciously provided me with an invaluable detailed commentary on almost every aspect of my analysis, with special emphasis on the *Pensées'* editorial history. Philippe Sellier has generously expressed his disagreement with some of my ideas, thus forcing me to defend my argument more cogently. Charles Natoli brought to my manuscript the much needed perspective of a philosopher steeped in Pascalian scholarship.

But most of all, I am truly honored and blessed in having two wonderful friends and colleagues, Jim Reid and Eric Gans, whose contribution to my work has been immeasurable. They possess an uncanny sense of knowing when to criticize, needle, and push and when to encourage and pull. We spent countless hours discussing Pascal's text and literary theory. They painstakingly read through several drafts of my manuscript and demonstrated true collegiality in the highest degree. Their intelligence and sensitivity commands my total admiration and gratitude.

And to my friends who encouraged me to continue when there seemed to be no light at the end of the proverbial tunnel, I say thank you. Lynn Mitchell, Brooke Barton, and Larry Kritzman encouraged me to pursue what often appeared to be a Sisyphean task. I owe special thanks to Paul Herstein who read major portions of the manuscript.

The manuscript completed, my work had just begun to transform it into a book with the University of California Press. Grace Stimson, a "creative" editor, deserves special mention for her excellent work on my manuscript. I wish to thank the entire Los Angeles office for their assistance, particularly Matthew Jaffe, who helped me in countless, much appreciated ways.

# Introduction

We have to cease to think if we refuse to do
it in the prison-house of language.

—Nietzsche

"Pascal's blood flows in my veins," wrote Nietzsche.[1] Indeed,
Pascal's blood flows in the veins of contemporary culture. The
*Pensées* present one of the major dilemmas that structures contemporary thought. This dilemma centers on the relationship between
knowledge of an absolute origin—God or a transcendent truth—
and human discourse, which threatens to undermine the very
possibility of knowing or representing an origin. Traditionally,
language is seen as a tool of knowledge, able to transcend itself
and represent God, the origin of knowledge.[2] In the wake of
Nietzsche, however, modern thought questions this traditional
view of the relation of language to truth. Modern critical theory,
in particular, reinterprets truth and reality as concepts derived
from, not discovered by, language. It argues that what we perceive
as truth is, in fact, given to us prereflectively by conventional
codes embedded in language; all our perceptions are mediated
and shaped by language. We do not apprehend the world itself,
but only representations of it in our signs. Trapped in a "prison-
house of language,"[3] we have no way of knowing whether these
signs correspond to a truth outside language.

The *Pensées* present the incompatible logics of both traditional
and modern views on language's relation to an origin, God. On
the one hand, the *Pensées* adopt a perspective of faith based on

1

the traditional notion that we can transcend language to know God. But on the other hand, they present an opposing perspective of uncertainty which, like modern critical theory, questions whether we are not trapped within human representations of reality and thus do not have access to reality itself. If it were possible to determine rationally the truth of either perspective, a wager would not be necessary. The wager lies at the heart of the *Pensées* precisely because the correctness of either one of its two perspectives is undecidable.

Whether or not one agrees with the Nietzschean legacy in contemporary critical theory, which reads texts by deciphering their warring factions and by locating their ultimate moment of undecidability, the *Pensées* do invite such a reading. As Lucien Goldmann argues, for Pascal all linguistic statements are neither completely certain nor uncertain, neither completely true nor false.[4] The undecidable nature of discourse, which necessarily includes the *Pensées* themselves, stems from Pascal's specific notion of the Fall and of a hidden God. Since Adam's Fall, God has become a *deus absconditus*, withdrawing his presence from the world and breaking off communication with humans as punishment for their sin: "This religion . . . consists in the belief that man is fallen from a state of glory and communication with God" ("Cette religion . . . consiste à croire que l'homme est déchu d'un état de gloire et de communication avec Dieu").[5] The Christian religion asserts that "men are in darkness and removed from God, that he has hidden himself from their knowledge, that this is even the very name he gives himself in the Scriptures, *Deus absconditus*" ("les hommes sont dans les ténèbres et dans l'éloignement de Dieu, qu'il s'est caché à leur connaissance, que c'est même le nom qu'il se donne dans les Ecritures, *Deus absconditus*" [S681, L427, B194]).[6] For Pascal, the Fall away from God brings about an epistemological fall—a fall from truth into language. Cut off from God and from the world of essential truth, we fall into a world of obscurity, of opaque signs.[7] It is impossible to know on the basis of these signs alone whether they show us the truth. If God does communicate with us, it is not through our purely conventional, intelligible signs. If he exists, he does not stand in a positive relation to the world and humankind: no *nomos*, no law of nature, emanates from him, and thus no certain guidelines for human existence. The hidden God reveals himself only in the negative experience of Otherness. God is the Unknown, the totally Other, incomprehensible in terms of any worldly analogies. "If there is a God, he is infinitely incomprehensible since, being indivisible and without limits, he bears no relation to us" ("S'il y a un Dieu, il est infiniment incompréhensible puisque, n'ayant ni parties ni bornes, il n'a nul rapport à nous" [S680, L418, B233]). Thus the "things of God [are] inexpressible" ("les choses de Dieu [sont] inexprimables" [S303, L272, B687]). If we are fallen into language, how then can we express and come to know the totally Other that lies outside human discourse?[8] How can we know whether our particular notions of God, the Fall, and Redemption are not just conventional codes produced by human discourse? Indeed, how can we even know whether God exists?

The Fall is thus central to the *Pensées* because it affects human discourse about God.[9] Pascal's notion of an epistemological fall from truth into language generates an aporia,* two irreconcilable interpretations, within his text.[10] And both interpretations focus on this fall from truth into language. In the perspective of faith,

---

*Aporia derives from the Greek word *aporos*, meaning an unpassable path or an impasse. According to *Webster's Third New International Dictionary*, it is a rhetorical term which designates "a problem or difficulty arising from an awareness of opposing or incompatible views on the same theoretic matter, especially one giving rise to philosophically systematic doubt."

Aporia has become a key concept in modern deconstructive theory because it reveals the ultimate impasse of philosophy's truth claims. For Paul de Man, philosophical reason is subverted by rhetoric; the figurative nature of all language gives rise to "at least two mutually exclusive readings and asserts the impossibility of a true understanding" (*Allegories of Reading* [New Haven: Yale University Press, 1979], p. 72). De Man explains his notion of an aporia as "the confrontation of incompatible meanings between which it is necessary but impossible to decide in terms of truth and error. If one of the readings is declared true, it will always be possible to undo it by means of the other; if it is decreed false, it will be possible to demonstrate that it states the truth of its aberration" (ibid., p. 76).

Historically, aporia has been used simply to designate a state of doubt or uncertainty. The *Oxford English Dictionary* offers an instance in which the aporetical is likened to the skeptical: "The greatest Wits of the World have been . . . Skeptical or Aporetical" (H. Moore, *Div. Dial.* IV.iii [1713]). Given this association, one might think that Pascal's use of an aporetic discourse is simply a special case of Pyrrhonism, about which he speaks at great length. I want to emphasize, however, that my use of the term "aporia" as applied to Pascal's discourse is not to be equated with doubt of Pyrrhonism. Pyrrhonism and aporia, as defined by modern deconstructive theory, presuppose two different modes of thought, two different relationships to notions or truth and error. Although Pyrrhonism may seem at

which is one side of the aporia, this fall is a consequence of the
historical Fall. Humankind fell from a state of communication
with God who guaranteed an unfallen, referential language: the
correspondence of signs to truth. Since the Fall, language has
become nonreferential and falls into figures that always state something other than what they directly mean; thus they cannot point
directly to a prefallen state. Although this otherness of figural language marks our fallen state, it also can hold the key to Redemption. Language not only points to the debasement of its representative capacity; it also suggests something other than its codes and
structures, something that they exclude. Pascal wagers that the
otherness within language itself figures God's Otherness, which
is outside language. The story of the Fall and Redemption implies
that its narrator has transcended language to acquire through
faith the certainty of God's existence.[11]

The viewpoint of faith, however, cannot account for the whole
of the Pascalian text. The *Pensées* engender another, incompatible
interpretation when they are seen from the perspective of uncertainty, the other side of the aporia. The historical Fall, paradoxically, places one in the position of being unable to say whether
a fall, in fact, even took place. A fall implies a pristine origin from
which one has fallen. Trapped in language, we can never transcend
our fallen state to know of such an origin from which we have
fallen. All that we can experience is a fall from the belief that our

first glance to suggest the undecidability, the uncertainty, of meaning with respect
to truth and error, it ultimately implies a position of truth: the uncertainty of
truth becomes a form of certainty. Pascal, however, is aware that the certainty
of uncertainty is an inverted form of the dogmatism that it opposes: " . . . it is
not certain that everything is uncertain" (S453, L521, B387). Pyrrhonism is an
epistemology that assumes the possibility of a logic that can describe what is
true—here the truth of uncertainty.

Aporia, in the modern deconstructive sense, is born of the knowledge that there
can be no certain knowledge. It brings to light the failure of our attempts to seize
the truth of the world. It presupposes a realm of reading situated in the interstices
of the ever-shifting poles of truth and error. Although a reading may at one
moment seem to have captured the truth, it becomes obvious in the next moment
that what it has acquired is only a representation of truth and not truth itself.
This recognition of error leads in turn to the construction of a new story which
can also be "deconstructed." To the extent that one can speak of truth in this
perspective, one can only describe the continual movement between readings of
truth and error.

signs correspond to truth. Thus, from the perspective of uncertainty, the fall from truth into language produces the story of the fall from the illusion that we can capture a truth.

Depending upon which side of the aporia we choose, one interpretation appears to incorporate the other. From the perspective of belief, the story of the Fall and Redemption can be made to subsume that of the fall from the belief in truth. The very recognition that our language is fallen points to a former state of perfection where we were in communication with God and truth. The realization of our imprisonment in language is a form of punishment to make us aware of our fallen condition. This awareness will lead us to wager for God's existence and accede to a new realm of understanding beyond language.

Conversely, the story of the fall from the belief in truth can be made to subsume the alternate story of the Fall and Redemption. From within the framework of uncertainty, the story of the Fall and Redemption does not necessarily represent events corresponding to an objective truth but may merely be a set of conventional structures that create an illusion of truth. Every effort to conceive of a Paradise where signs corresponded with truth, an absolute origin from which we have fallen, leads back only to a conventional, and thus misleading, sign of the origin.

Neither interpretation can succeed in its attempt to subsume the other because Pascal[12] keeps shifting the perspective. Every time we assume the truth of one story of the fall, we find ourselves inescapably falling into its opposite: " . . . at the end of each truth, it is necessary to add that we bear in mind the opposite truth" (" . . . à la fin de chaque vérité il faut ajouter qu'on se souvient de la vérité opposée" [S479, L576, B567]). Both interpretations appear true and yet both seem false when one adopts the opposite perspective. This aporia accounts for the controversy among Pascalian scholars, who adopt either one interpretive framework or the other and perceive the one chosen as the "truth" of the text. Indeed, the polarization dates back to the original Port-Royal readers who established the first edition. What are now known as the *Pensées* initially had no form or title; the first editors entitled them "M. Pascal's Thoughts on Religion and other Subjects," clearly indicating that they interpreted the collection of fragments as the story of faith, one that subsumed all the other thoughts.

And indeed, their editing of the text itself sought to expunge the most objectionable traces of the Fall: doubt and uncertainty. Voltaire's *Remarques sur les Pensées de Pascal* (1734) and Condorcet's edition of the *Pensées* (1776) focused on the other side of the aporia by separating out the philosophic thoughts from the religious ones. Both Voltaire and Condorcet emphasized the perspective of uncertainty at the expense of the perspective of belief.

Modern readings of the *Pensées* tend to be divided along the same general lines. Many critics, reading the text from the viewpoint of faith,[13] seek to rise above the limitations imposed by the language of the text—its elliptical and unfinished phrases, its fragmentary structure—to decipher what they believe to be the totalizing meaning contained in the text. Others, however, without taking an explicit stand on the issue, implicitly treat the *Pensées* as a fallen text, for they discuss it as a *divertissement*, as a work of literature and poetry.[14] They focus on the aesthetic aspects of the *Pensées* as fragments and relegate the theological and historical arguments to a secondary place.

The *Pensées* leave us with the undecidability of an aporia because we have fallen away not only from God, a *deus absconditus*, but also from Pascal, a *homo absconditus*, who has hidden his text. In composing the *Pensées*, Pascal literally cut up his text with a scissors, separating one thought from the text. He died, however, before he could reorder all the various fragments. As a result the *Pensées* do not present themselves as a whole but as a cross-current of amorphous notes, personal and impulsive jottings mixed with highly developed thoughts, 40 percent of them loosely classified into twenty-eight titled *liasses*. Pascal's gesture of fragmenting his thoughts highlights, perhaps unwittingly, the absence of a unified reading or intention by cutting his text off from his authorial truth.

Given that Pascal is a *homo absconditus* whose true design is hidden from his text and from his reader, the traditional reading of the *Pensées* as an apology for the Christian religion must be seriously questioned. Edouard Morot-Sir first challenged the notion of the *Pensées* as an apology by noting that the word "apology" does not even appear once in Pascal's text.[15] He further observed that neither Gilberte Pascal nor Etienne Périer used the word to designate the disassembled notes of their brother and uncle. Regarding these notes, Morot-Sir rightly asks whether we should attempt to reconstitute "the work that will never be written."[16] He suggests that the manuscript, which he characterizes as "fragments for a future work,"[17] provides a model of all language. Signs point only to a future meaning that can never be decided upon. If such is the case, the signs of the text cannot clearly point to an apology, at least not in the traditional sense of the word.

The *Pensées* are constituted by an aporetic discourse which forces the readers to question the very possibility of a human apology. The basic assumption underlying an apology is the controlling presence of an author's intention to persuade the reader of a truth.[18] Moreover, an apologetic discourse presupposes a belief in the persuasive force of language; language is capable of expressing, either explicitly or implicitly, what the author intends. An apologetic discourse and an aporetic discourse are thus mutually exclusive. The former asserts that it can communicate a clear, unambiguous meaning capable of transcending language's fall from truth. In this perspective, the story of faith would ultimately subsume that of uncertainty, since the latter implies that the ultimate meaning cannot be decided in terms of truth and falsity. An aporetic discourse, however, does not mean that the story of uncertainty incorporates that of faith, for uncertainty is itself uncertain. The aporetic discourse of the *Pensées* suggests that the signs that constitute it do not point clearly to either story. The text's true reading cannot be contained in any of its signs.

My ultimate goal in this book is to explore the problem of reading signs in a world where one has fallen away from the certainty of an origin, be it that of Pascal, the human author, or that of God, the divine Author. In such a world, one has fallen away from the comforting epistemological categories of truth and error and is left simply with a series of readings, with the ways in which each reading can capture only fragments and thus misrepresents the truth. My study focuses on Pascal's view of the Fall as affecting language and reading. The Fall is a story about language and reading. The *Pensées* establish a model of interpretation which brings together but does not reconcile the two sides of the aporia.[19] It induces its readers to recognize the impossibility of discovering its true meaning, by stating indirectly that its signs cannot transcend their fallen status. Indeed, it rejects the notion that a rational decision can determine whether any given interpretation is true, which would be an act of pride.[20] True understanding comes not from pridefully seeking to read a rational, objective meaning buried in the signs of a text, but from recognizing how all readings fail to seize truth. The *Pensées'* aporia makes the readers constantly fall from their prideful illusion that their understanding of the text captures its truth or original intention. But the very story of the fall from illusion is itself an allegory of the historical Fall. In making the readers aware that they are always misrepresenting the text's true meaning, the *Pensées* open them up to another method of reading the historical Fall, one that has no story, for it theoretically takes place through the heart, which, like God, is outside time and language. Only in this way can the readers open themselves up to a God who can read through them by projecting his unity and meaning onto their hearts. God communicates with humans not by presenting them with signs in a text but by acting as a hidden author, who through the heart, which is atextual, enables them to read a truth the text cannot contain.

Thus, although the *Pensées* fall into an aporia, it does not follow that Pascal abandons his search to communicate a transcendent truth. Unlike Nietzsche and modern critical theorists, Pascal belongs to that group of individuals who, according to Derrida's famous characterization, do not experience "the joyous affirmation of the freeplay of the world . . . without truth, without origin," but rather have "dreams of deciphering a truth or an origin which is free from freeplay and from the order of the sign, and lives like an exile the necessity of interpretation."[21] But Pascal believes, as does Derrida, that such dreams are impossible within the limits of human life because any attempt to decode a truth or an origin will be a product of the particular code one chooses. Pascal thus seeks a solution outside language; he wagers to go beyond textuality through the heart, the atextual origin of certainty.

# 1

# Seventeenth-Century Discourse: Sin and Signs

The notion of the Fall lies at the heart of seventeenth-century theories of language. Many of the treatises on language evoke the doctrine of the Fall or of Original Sin, either explicitly or implicitly.[1] For example, Sénault, a seventeenth-century theoretician, writes in *L'Homme criminel:* "Since nature is criminal, one should not be surprised that its language is corrupt."[2] The evocation of the Fall was necessary to account for what was perceived as the fundamental flaw in language, that signs are separated from the real world to which they refer. According to the modern critic Pierre Kuentz, Christian doctrine provides a framework within which this defect can be understood: "Christian dogma furnishes the original gap that allows one to postulate both the gap and its negation at the same time. It postulates, in effect, the foundation of rhetorical structure, an initial transgression, a faulty first step, an original discrepancy."[3] The seventeenth-century treatises on language illustrate what Jacques Derrida sees as a major phenomenon of Western thought: the attribution of the gaps in human sign systems to the concept of the Fall. In Derrida's words, "absence and the sign always seem to make an apparent, provisional, and derivative notch in the system of first and last presence. They are thought as accidents and not as conditions of the desired presence. The sign is always a sign of the Fall. Absence always relates

9

to distancing from God."[4] The theological notion of the Fall thus informs human language.

The seventeenth century was witness to an unusual profusion of treatises on language, many of them encouraged by the founding of the French Academy in 1635.[5] Richelieu, its first patron, certainly wanted the French language and literature to be free of any traces of the Fall or of Original Sin. The official linguistic and literary goals of the Academy were to be compatible with Richelieu's lofty ambitions for the monarchy. Richelieu thus sought to encourage the development of an official grammar, rhetoric, poetics, and of a dictionary, all guided by the principles of *pureté* and *netteté* of language. These principles sought, in effect, to remove from consciousness the existence of the gaps that separate signs from objects to create the impression of truth and control. Not all the seventeenth-century treatises on language, however, were spawned by the Academy; in fact, many were opposed to its ideology.

Two opposing attitudes regarding the separation between signs and objects are thus found in seventeenth-century discourse, but both derive from theological principles. Classicism, supported by the ideology of the state and by Cartesian thought, strives to eradicate or minimize the split, seeking, in effect, an unfallen discourse. Classical discourse[6] thus develops a semiological system to codify and control the relationship between words and things. But, unlike modern semiology, it assumes that the tendency of language to conform to a code is an accurate indication of its truthfulness. In opposition to classical ideology, the Barcosian faction of Jansenism, which includes Pascal, seeks, rather, to maximize the gap in order to eradicate the illusion that an unfallen discourse is possible. The Barcosian and Pascalian discourse attempts to subvert the semiological code by showing that all language is inherently figural (rhetorical). Rhetorical language is irredeemably fallen because figures disrupt the one-to-one relationship between words and things by introducing alternative and contradictory meanings. Meaning is always other than what language directly states.

My goal in this chapter is to show how seventeenth-century discourse was struggling between a semiological and a rhetorical

approach to language.* Because Pascal was acutely aware of the
relationship between language and the Fall, dramatizing and integrating it into the *Pensées,* he was able to perceive what modern
semiologists have articulated: language misrepresents the outside
world and points to its own structures which suggest meanings
other than those they intend. Unlike modern semiologists, however, Pascal believes that one must go further, for language's self-
reference is not sufficient to explain everything that language
does. For Pascal, as for poststructuralists, language not only fig-

---

*My distinction here between semiology and rhetoric is based on Paul de Man's
discussion, "Semiology and Rhetoric," in *Allegories of Reading* (New Haven: Yale
University Press, 1979), pp. 3–19. According to de Man, literary semiology, as it
has been used by theorists such as Barthes, Genette, Todorov, and Greimas,
employs grammatical (especially syntactical) structures as if they were basically
similar to rhetorical structures. For these theorists, grammar and rhetoric operate
in perfect continuity; it is possible to pass from one structure to another without
any problem.

De Man, however, argues that semiology and rhetoric are not continuous but
constitute two different disciplines, with the latter putting the former into question.
Semiology is generally viewed as "the science of signs." The word "science" implies
that one can describe objectively the way in which signs function. It is possible
to understand the functioning of signs by studying their grammar, the logic of
how signs are linked. Grammar "postulates the possibility of unproblematic,
dyadic meaning" (p. 9); it assumes a one-to-one equivalence between signs and
meaning. Logic establishes "a consistent link between sign and meaning that
operates within grammatical patterns" (p. 8). Logic "postulates the possibility of
the universal truth of meanings" (p. 9). The notion of a semiology, then, presupposes that there is a logical construct, a structure of structures which can accurately
represent the text and show how its signs operate.

De Man's use of the term "rhetoric" does not designate the traditional discipline
of the art of persuasion or eloquence. Rather, it refers to the study of tropes and
figures. For de Man, tropes and figures suspend logic and semiological structures,
thus opening up "vertiginous possibilities of referential aberration" (p. 10). Tropes
and figures cannot be controlled by grammatical models, a subset of semiological
structures, as they contain a wild card that can unpredictably throw open another
arena of unforeseen meaning. Thus one cannot decide "by grammatical or other
linguistic devices" which of the competing meanings dominates (p. 10).

For de Man, tropes and figures are not ornaments, as the Aristotelian tradition
would have it, but constitute the very basis of language. He situates his discussion
partly within the context of Kenneth Burke's work which also questions the
continuity between grammar and rhetoric. Burke characterizes tropes and figures
by the term "displacement," which he compares with Freudian displacement,
defined as "any slight bias or even unintended error" (p. 10). The deflective
character of rhetoric subverts "the consistent link between sign and meaning"
upon which semiology is predicated.

ures the otherness within language itself; it also figures something other than itself. This otherness within language leaves open the possibility of both a divine and a nondivine reading. And this otherness, Pascal would wager, figures God's Otherness, outside of language.

## CARTESIAN RATIONALISM AND UNFALLEN CLASSICAL DISCOURSE

Confronted by the split between signs and the world to which they refer, Cartesian rationalists aspire to transcend the fallen status of human discourse and to develop a language completely adequate to thought and truth. Descartes dreams of conquering Babel and the fall of language through the creation of an exact, universal language that would guard against error. A language that guaranteed an accurate representation of truth would render humans "the masters and possessors of nature."[7] In a letter to Mersenne, Descartes writes: "In the future, I would dare hope for a universal language that would be easy to learn, pronounce, and write, and, more important still, a language that would help us to improve our judgment by representing all things so clearly that making a mistake would be almost impossible; this language would guard against words that have only confused meanings to which men's minds have become so accustomed, producing imperfect understanding."[8] Descartes maintains that such a language is possible and that "peasants could better judge the true nature of things than philosophers do now" because they can discover the "science" that underlies language.[9]

This belief presupposes firm confidence in the ability of signs to capture and represent a real world fully without leaving any gaps. Timothy Reiss writes that, for Descartes, "language reveals thought, and in so far as it refers to objects it can operate as a perfect stand-in for them. It is not, to be sure, the object itself; but it is conceived of as a sufficiently accurate representation for the purposes of discourse, into whose system it may be inserted."[10] Yet language, as Descartes noted, does not always operate as a perfect stand-in for thought. The success of language as an instrument of knowledge depends on its ability to create a close resemblance between word and thought, to substitute one for the other. Thus, for Descartes, language is not inextricably rooted in sin; it does not distort pure thought: "a Frenchman and a German" may have "the same thoughts or reasonings concerning the same things although they conceive of them with entirely different words."[11] Language does not contaminate thought with its mediating force. Rather, it may be viewed as a lever hoisting up the mind into realms that would otherwise remain inaccessible. In order to reach such heights, language must not weigh upon thought with any indications of itself. Having achieved its goal, language should fade into oblivion, not leaving any residue to distract meaning and lead it onto competing paths. Classical discourse thus values clarity, transparence, concision.

Descartes' ideal language implies a semiological system that subordinates rhetoric to a logical code.[12] The semiological code is an attempt to fix and control meaning by establishing a one-to-one relationship between signifier and signified, a connection the Cartesians confused with a one-to-one relationship between sign and referent. Although this Cartesian binary code does allow for figural meaning, it too must be carefully coded and controlled. One signifier may be substituted for another, but only if it does not produce more than one clear and distinct signified. In the event that two signifieds are produced, the logical code situates them in a hierarchy, subordinating the secondary one to the main one so that it cannot threaten the primary signified's meaning. In this way figures are reduced to mere ornaments that are tolerated as long as they do not impinge on the clarity of thought.

Ultimately, the semiological, classical view of language attempts nothing less than the reversal of our fallen condition. It is based, in Derridean terms, on a "Metaphysics of Presence," which holds that a full truth lies behind every sign. It seeks a moment of original plenitude when language and thought simultaneously present themselves to our consciousness. In this moment of truth, when language and thought are completely united, language becomes superfluous, for it has already accomplished its transportational function. It then slips away, leaving only the full presence of meaning. Through this longing for limpid clarity, for an unmediated world, the classical ideal strives to recreate an unfallen world.

*Classicism and the Eclipse of Rhetoric*

Seeking control of language, thought, and truth, classicism must therefore try to dismantle rhetoric, which threatens to undermine that control. The traditional *trivium,* rhetoric, logic, and grammar, became a *bivium;* rhetoric was radically diminished and basically absorbed by the categories of its sister disciplines.[13] To the extent that rhetoric still existed as a science in the seventeenth century, it had lost the scope and stature of its Aristotelian ancestor. In the Aristotelian tradition, rhetoric was the art of persuasion and it included five categories: *inventio, dispositio, elocutio, pronuntiatio,* and *memoria.* The seventeenth century, however, had no need for the last two categories, *pronuntiatio* and *memoria,* because public oration was moribund and had become less prevalent than written discourse.[14] The Port-Royal *Logique ou l'Art de penser* and *Grammaire générale et raisonnée* struck the crucial deathblow to *inventio* and *dispositio* by replacing them with logic and grammar.[15] Arnauld and Nicole argue that an art or a method of invention and expression is superfluous because natural facility and common usage are adequate for persuasion. The cultivation of art only leads one astray by fostering false and hyperbolic thoughts, forced figures, and other defects of the rhetorical style. *Elocutio* was the sole survivor of this assault and thus rhetoric was reduced to the study of tropes and figures. But even the use of tropes and figures was to be restrained. The linguistic treatises of the seventeenth century, railing against the danger tropes and figures posed to clarity, concluded that they should be relegated to the benign realm of decoration where they might ennoble thought without affecting it. As ornamental devices, they might be a source of external beauty without touching the internal substance.

The attempt to restrain rhetoric stemmed from a profound mistrust of language's powers to represent or, more precisely, from the suspicion that rhetoric misrepresents thought. This fear of deception harks back to the oldest condemnations of the rhetorical capacity of language. The discipline of rhetoric was born, Roland Barthes reminds us,[16] in the law courts of Syracuse in 485 B.C. The disputes arbitrated in the courts concerned events that took place in the past. Given the irreversibility of time, it was impossible to reenact those events, and one had to seek recourse in another medium: language. Words, uttered in the present, came to substitute themselves for past events. The function of words was to render present this past and hence to enable the present listeners, the jury, to decide on the just and true solution of the past conflict. The discipline of rhetoric developed out of this need to persuade the jurors that certain grammatical statements were true. It was quickly observed, however, that rhetoric was equally capable of persuading people that false as well as correct statements were true. Rhetoric's duplicity, for example, led to Plato's severe indictment of the discipline. In the *Gorgias*, Socrates criticized its eponymous character and the Sophists in general for using language to manipulate the perception of truth. Rhetoric is suspect because "by the power of language, one can make unimportant things seem important and reciprocally one can make important things seem unimportant."[17] Rhetoric has little regard for truth: "the true-seeming is as good as the true."[18]

In the strengths of rhetoric, therefore, lay the seeds of its own undoing or, at the very least, the grounds for mistrust. Because, as Paul Ricoeur notes, rhetoric is the power to arrange and manipulate words in the absence of things,[19] it implies a radical separation of words from things. Pushed to their extreme, words may liberate themselves completely from the object they are supposed to designate. Although the discipline of rhetoric originally posited that rhetoric served truth, that ideal was not always adhered to in practice. Words, so easily detachable from things, may rebel; they need not reflect an outside truth but need only concern themselves with the appearance of truth.

Although throughout history rhetoric has been traditionally attacked because it could serve as a willful, conscious means of distorting the truth, the seventeenth century found a new ground of attack. Descartes, for example, focuses on the involuntary, unconscious meanderings of thought which may lead one astray, bringing out the latent imprecision and unseen deceptiveness of language. Descartes, in his *Discourse on Method*, expresses his reservations about publishing his work because his language, which may escape his conscious control and express other meanings, may betray him: "I have often explained some of my opinions to people of good mind, and who, while I was speaking to them, seemed to understand most distinctly, yet, when they repeated these opinions, I have noticed that they almost always change them in such a way that I could no longer acknowledge them as mine."[20] Although Descartes distrusts ordinary and literary language, he does have a new, humanistic optimism that people can purify and rectify language by their own efforts, based on scientific principles of clear and precise definitions, and thus solve the problem of representation.

### Vaugelas and Bouhours

The fear of the uncontrollable nature of rhetoric was not limited to Descartes; it affected many of the seventeenth-century theoreticians of language. For example, Vaugelas and Bouhours, two of the most influential theoreticians of classical language, judged rhetorical figures suspect because of their ability to turn our attention away from the truth. Figures introduce an opacity into language which produces secondary meanings, thus troubling the exact correspondence between words and thought. Like Descartes, Vaugelas's and Bouhours's distrust of rhetoric implies belief and confidence in a nonrhetorical or purely semiological language able to produce univocal meaning and to serve as an instrument of truth. Their goal is to purify language, to guarantee its adequacy to thought and truth by divesting it of rhetorical contaminating agents. According to Vaugelas, to write with *netteté*, one of the chief virtues of classical language, is to write "so clearly and intelligibly in all areas, expressing oneself so well that the reader will immediately be able to grasp the author's intention."[21] Language is capable of clearly communicating the author's intention so long as it is not troubled by figures that all too often introduce equivocal or unclear meanings. Bouhours also has confidence in the ability of the French language to express thought adequately.[22] "Thoughts . . . are mental images of things, as words are images of thoughts; in general, to think is to create a mental image of a spiritual or material object. But mental images are true only if they resemble their object: thus a thought is true if it represents things faithfully; it is false if it recreates them differently from what they truly are."[23]

Yet, despite Vaugelas's and Bouhours's belief in a transparent language that can resemble its objects, rhetoric is still perceived as necessary. *Netteté* and *pureté* alone do not suffice; also needed are "elegance, softness, majesty, and strength and all that results from them, to musicality and grace,"[24] which come from rhetorical figures. Rhetoric is called upon to supplement language: "Since this language cannot give to things an appropriate air, it adorns and decorates them as much as possible."[25]

Because figures cannot be completely eliminated, Vaugelas, Bouhours, and other theoreticians of the seventeenth century developed the classical doctrine of language which, in keeping with Cartesian ideology, seeks to subordinate figures to a semiological system. They domesticate figures by setting forth elaborate rules to codify their use. Meaning should be transparent and immediately accessible, so that readers will not be distracted by misleading paths. Figures, in this classical perspective, are reduced to tame ornaments, detachable devices used to give greater elegance and emotional impact to thought without affecting its meaning. Equivocations, for example, are banned because they are not ornaments but simple defects. An equivocation "is not always easy to understand; its double meaning gives it a mysterious appearance and renders access to its true meaning arduous."[26] The capacity of rhetorical figures to produce a doubleness of meaning is what threatens the referential capacity of language. Figures are therefore permitted only to the extent that their double meaning can easily be reduced to a single one; "metaphors are like transparent veils that let us see what they cover; they are like costumes beneath which we recognize the disguised person."[27] Because metaphors, like all figures, threaten to introduce a second meaning, they should be used only when there is no other way of expressing the same idea and only in such a way that the one correct meaning is immediately available. The correctness of metaphorical meaning is determined by conventional usage: "As for metaphor, [language] uses it only when it cannot do without it, or when metaphors, through extensive use, have become the proper term. It particularly cannot tolerate metaphors that are too daring."[28] Similarly, hyperboles are permitted only under the condition that usage has worn down the sharp edges and naturalized them: "there are less daring hyperboles, ones that do not extend beyond the limits of common usage, although they do go beyond common belief. There are some that usage has naturalized, so to speak, and they are so well established that they do not shock."[29] When convention has failed to domesticate hyperboles, the text itself must supply sufficient indications to prepare the reader to make the proper interpretive leap: "As for those that are progressively introduced in the text, they do not disturb the readers."[30] The readers should not be jolted by the sudden intervention of a new element that cannot be easily assimilated into the old framework. Otherwise, an interpretive act would be required which might carry them away from the text's originating pulse.

Although these treatises align themselves with the classical ideology that seeks to establish a semiological code to control the figurative capacity of representational language, at the same time they inadvertently suggest the possibility that there may exist a gap separating all language, not just certain figures, from the real world to which it refers. Why would such intricate rules about representation be necessary if there were not some deep-seated fear of misrepresentation? All language does indeed have the power to obscure and deceive. Does it deceive us into believing that we can escape deception? Vaugelas and Bouhours would respond in the negative, but their writings inadvertently pose questions about the adequacy of language. These questions are raised implicitly by the theories of Arnauld and Nicole and explicitly by opposing theories of rhetoric, such as those proposed by Barcos and Pascal.

### Arnauld, Nicole, La Logique *of Port-Royal:*<br>*The Struggle between Semiology and Rhetoric*

The struggle to subordinate rhetoric to semiological structures is intensified in the work of Arnauld and Nicole. Influenced not only by Descartes but also by Pascal, they were drawn in opposite directions.[31] Like Descartes, they are confident that language can be made adequate to thought and truth. They seek to develop a semiological system that posits a fixed code providing a logic to link sign to meaning in a direct, clear way. Yet their discussion of sign systems, which betrays a distinct Pascalian influence, suggests inadvertently that semiology may fall into an untrustworthy figural language. Figures point to two signifieds which may be incompatible with each other, rendering the true meaning undecidable. Such figures would subvert the clarity and control of classical language.

Like Descartes and the classical tradition, Arnauld and Nicole seek a language consonant with thought. They favor the development of a dictionary of meanings which would take the form of a grammar. The grammar and logic upon which the dictionary would be based are designed to institutionalize and regulate the coding and decoding of meaning. A carefully coded language is a controlled language.

Since their goal is to tighten the links among language, thought, and truth, it is not surprising that Arnauld and Nicole are also basically hostile to rhetoric:

> The mind provides sufficient thoughts; usage furnishes the expressions; as for rhetorical figures and ornaments, there are always too many. So everything consists in eliminating the bad ways of writing and speaking, especially an artificial and rhetorical style composed of hyperbolic, wrong thoughts, and false figures, which are the worst vice of all.[32]

Common usage and the natural facility of the mind should replace the art of rhetoric, *inventio* and *dispositio*. Artifice, an unnecessary and potentially dangerous supplement, may impede the clear presentation of truth. Rhetorical figures may rupture what might otherwise be perceived as a closed chain linking words to meaning. Figures may break down the supposed one-to-one relationship between signifier and signified by introducing competing signifieds that cannot simply be placed in a harmonious hierarchy. Since it may be difficult, if not impossible, to decide upon the correct signified, meaning might go haywire, suggesting more than is intended. For this reason Arnauld and Nicole favor a neutral style, one that will keep a tighter rein on meanings that might wander astray.

In order to permit, yet restrain, the use of figures, Arnauld and Nicole develop a theory of figural language based on what they call principal and accessory meanings. They set up a hierarchy of three different kinds of meanings produced by figural language. Each word first and foremost communicates a proper or main idea "which one regards as the proper meaning of this word."[33] In addition to this principal idea, words conjure up accessory ideas and figurative meanings which are of two kinds. The first is drawn from common usage which endows words with conventional connotations. For example, the expression "you lied," in addition to its principal meaning of "you know that the opposite of what you said is true," also conjures up "a notion of disdain or offense."[34] Because this first level of accessory ideas basically corresponds to "common usage," Arnauld and Nicole believe that communication with readers can be controlled by a conventional coding and decoding. Yet they describe a second level of accessory meanings which, though also drawn from common usage, may shade off into the periphery of that range, in remote regions unimagined by the author. These accessory ideas can be conveyed, for example, by the author's method of presentation: "they are probably . . . triggered by the tone of voice, by the appearance of the face, by gestures, and by other natural signs which link an infinity of ideas to our words, which diversify, change, diminish, and add to the meaning of words by attributing the image of movements, judgments, and opinions to the speaker."[35] The individual quirks of the speaker or of the reader may produce, as Arnauld and Nicole note, an infinite number of accessory ideas that may change one's perception of the main idea. As the accessory ideas may be infinite, the reader may choose the wrong conventional meaning or may in fact select an unconventional one.

Although Arnauld and Nicole's codification of language is an attempt to control its figural function, their codes lay open the possibility of figural meanings that cannot be contained within logic and grammar. Despite the fact that the private accessory ideas may be linked to the main one in the author's mind, the same association of ideas is not necessarily maintained during its transmission to the readers. Accessory ideas can be dislodged from their associative network, thus allowing the readers to reassemble them according to their own needs.

What drives a wedge between the author's and the readers' accessory ideas is the infinite that lurks in the background of *La Logique* as well as of the *Pensées*. The infinite provokes a complex real world that stimulates the search for ever new accessory signifieds to account for it:

> Although the air surrounding us changes at any given time, we consider it as always the same; we say it has turned from cold to warm as if it were the same, although often the air we feel as cold is not different from the one we found warm.[36]

> We consider animals' bodies and speak of them as if they were
> always the same, although we are not sure that after a few years
> there remains any part of the initial tissues that composed them.[37]

The signifiers "air" and "animals' bodies" keep the same signified although the world and objects to which they refer are in flux. Language is based on an illusion. The signifiers refer at every moment to a slightly modified real world; we speak, however, as if the main meaning always refers to the same world. The illusion that there is only one primary meaning attached to each signifier is necessary to guarantee some degree of communication. If we were to be more accurate and indicate at every turn the precise way in which the world to which "air" or "animals' bodies" refers has changed, we would become mired in infinite modifications so that it would be impossible to continue with the rest of the sentence. We can indicate simple distinctions: "ordinary language permits us to say: this animal's body was composed of certain tissues ten years ago; now it is composed of entirely different ones."[38] But any effort at sharper precision would hinder, not help, communication, for it would serve only to cast doubt upon one's use of language. "There seems to be a contradiction in this discourse for, if all the parts are completely different, it should not be the same body."[39]

The problems that arise from Arnauld and Nicole's analysis of language are highly complex, yet Arnauld and Nicole ignore them. After suggesting the possibility of infinite connotations, they suddenly make it appear as if these connotations are always subordinated to a limited number of conventional denotations. They give no reason for stopping at this artificial limit. They do not explain why the accessory signifieds, in an effort to account for a constantly changing referential world, do not multiply infinitely. *La Logique* thus inadvertently echoes the famous Heraclitean question: "Talking about a river, we also say that the water was muddy two days ago, and now it is crystal clear. Yet it is hardly the same water."[40] Arnauld and Nicole's theory of a transparent language forces them to ignore the consequences of their own remarks. Such an awareness of the multiple accessory meanings would threaten the authority of the principal meaning. Main ideas give unity to the communication process, but they do not necessarily correspond to the real world. Given an infinite flux in the real world, it might be possible for an accessory idea to become the principal idea and thus reduce the principal one to accessory status. In that event main meanings would be vulnerable to subversive figurative interpretations.

The Port-Royal *Logique* implicitly recognizes the subversive implications of its own theory of language, for it focuses on those points where meaning threatens to overflow the coded boundaries of language. It then tries to show, in a recuperative gesture, how this meaning can be contained and brought back within the order and control of language. *La Logique* indicates the various interpretive operations necessary to bring language into harmony with thought.

*La Logique* describes two complementary ways of coding and decoding language. Coding is necessitated by the very structure of language. Arnauld and Nicole view language as "the abridged version" of signifieds and referents. In other words, because not all signifiers and signifieds that are necessary to express the thought completely can be present in a linguistic sequence, language has gaps. Language seeks an economy of words in order not to clutter up the communication process.[41] As a result, many expressions and meanings are omitted. Arnauld and Nicole give relative clauses as examples of complex expressions that are frequently not articulated because the same meaning can be communicated without them.

Since what is meant can never be totally translated into what is expressed, the utterance calls for an interpretive act. The readers must decipher the shared meanings encoded within language in order to "fill in everything that is not expressed."[42] Upon reading the phrase, "a transparent body," the readers easily transform this shorter expression into "a body that is transparent," the same but a longer expression. Arnauld and Nicole explain that "if this relative pronoun is not always expressed, it is always understood in some way."[43] The fact that language relies on many ideas that are implied shows that meaning depends on supplementary ideas stored in the readers' mind.[44]

Interpretation involves several kinds of substitution. At the most basic level it requires a mechanical replacement of one concept or expression for another. For example, the demonstrative pronoun *hoc* (this) replaces a noun for which the readers must mentally substitute the proper concept. In most instances the concept is supplied explicitly by the text itself. But the interpretive process may depart from textual indications and invite the readers to add to what is suggested on the printed page: "the mind *adds* to the precise meaning of terms" (emphasis added).[45] A sequence may encourage the readers to join to the stated noun certain unstated attributes: " . . . thus when one uses the term 'this one' to designate a diamond, the mind not only conceives of it as a concrete thing but adds to it the idea of a hard and brilliant object that has such a form."[46] The readers do not wait passively for the fullness of an already constructed meaning to impose itself; rather they must engage actively in gathering together the pertinent attributes that give meaning to the demonstrative pronoun's object:

> That is the reason why, according to the uses of the word *hoc* in various contexts, our mental additions are different. If I say *hoc* while pointing to a diamond, it will still mean *this thing*, but the mind will bridge the gap and add, which is a diamond, which is a hard and brilliant object; if it is wine, the mind will add to it the ideas of liquidity, taste, and color, and so with other things.[47]

Although the connotations are already encoded by the grammar of common usage, the readers' interpretive process does require selections. What ideas do readers choose to associate with the wine? Their choices will, of course, be determined by the context of the passage and by conventional associations. The readers will also, however, supplement these associations with others that may not correspond to conventional usage. Arnauld and Nicole recognize that words may trigger meanings not intended by the speaker, for "words often mean more than they seem to and when we want to explain their meanings, we do not capture all the impressions they imprint on our minds."[48] In using the word "wine," the author may intend to evoke the accessory ideas of "liquidity, taste, and color," but the readers may choose to attach to this word other conventional meanings.

Thus Arnauld and Nicole's solution for closing the gap between language and meaning creates other gaps. Although the readers are to rely on the shared meanings within language to fill in the gaps, it is possible that they will have recourse to other unintended conventional accessory meanings which may subvert the clarity of the semiological system. And although these interpretive operations are coded, the conventions are never sufficient to account for all the possibilities in an infinite world. Once the words leave the author's mind to find existence on the written page, they undergo the initial stage of separation. On the page, they enter the mainstream of circulation. No longer tied to the author's original meaning, they may evoke other unintended meanings contained in the linguistic system and in the mind of the reader. Language cannot always be controlled by the individual; it is the common property of the community at large.

Arnauld and Nicole are exploring the relation of language to thought, not in order to show the importance of the reader in the interpretive process but to present an interpretive model for certain elliptical theological statements. The most important statement, "This is my body," seems absurd on the surface. It does make sense when viewed as an abbreviation for "This is bread at this moment, this is my body at this other moment." How is the first sentence transformed into the second? The transformation takes place in the readers' mind, which must perform specific operations. Their ability to perform such operations depends on the mastery of the linguistic conventions that underlie discourse. As a first step, the readers must realize that the sentence, "This is my body," calls for interpretation by virtue of its incompleteness. The perception of incompleteness comes not from an understanding of language as a set of formal rules but from a general literary competence that provides models of meaning. Once the readers perceive the need for interpretation, they find the necessary meanings in a shared dogma. The competent readers know that the antecedent of the demonstrative pronoun *hoc* can be double. In this instance it refers to bread and to the body of Christ. Armed with this knowledge, "the mind adds to it clear and distinct ideas."[49] Jesus Christ pronounced the ambiguous word "this." The listeners, here the Apostles, possessing linguistic competence, knew they had to decipher the object to which he was referring. Thus in their minds they supplied the missing reference, "which is bread." This indication was not sufficient, for they knew that the conventions of meaning also required a time specification.

They thus further added, "this which is bread at this particular moment." They remembered that "this" was now being made to refer to the body of Christ and added a time specification to that meaning of the word, "this was his body at that particular moment." In this way they added incidental clauses to explicate the meaning of the words.

In spite of Arnauld and Nicole's interest in the problem of interpretation, their example illustrates the central role played by the readers in transforming the abbreviated sentence into a full one. The appropriate transformation is achieved by a series of potentially subversive additions made by readers who follow up the indications left by the author. Given the possibility that readers may stray too far from the author's intention, Arnauld and Nicole wanted to limit their role in the reading process by insisting that there is only one right way in which to "add" to the text. But their discussion of language nonetheless lays the theoretical groundwork for more leeway in interpretation. The leeway is much more evident in the discussions of ordinary language than in theological discourse; nonetheless, it is present there too.

Despite Arnauld and Nicole's desire to subordinate rhetoric to semiology, they do admit the necessity of rhetoric in some instances. Although a neutral style is most appropriate for the communication of human truths, divine knowledge must be conveyed through figures. When talking about divine truths, "the naked truth" does not suffice:

> . . . it is a mistake to talk about them in a dry and cold fashion because it is a mistake not to be touched by what should touch us. And so divine truths were not simply given to be known but more to be loved, revered, and adored by mankind; there is no doubt that the noble, high, and figured way with which the Holy Fathers treated them is much more appropriate to them than the simple and figureless style used by the Scholastics. . . . the scholastic style was simple and held only the ideas of the naked truth; it is therefore less able to produce within the soul the movements of respect and love we must give to Christian truths.[50]

Figures are capable not only of the highest truths but also of the lowest and most frightening truth about language itself. In order to achieve their highest end, figures should be contained within the bounds delineated by the theory of principal and accessory ideas. This theory, however, is set against the background of the infinite universe which causes meaning to seep through its containers, overflowing the bounds of the neat distinction between principal and accessory meanings. Thus, although figures are designed to point to the possibility of Redemption, they may uncontrollably also take a wrong turn and point to the Fall.

## JANSENISM (THE BARCOSIAN FACTION) AND FALLEN DISCOURSE

Contrary to many discussions that tend simply to equate Jansenism with the thought of Arnauld and Nicole, Jansenism is not a monolithic unit.[51] Arnauld and Nicole's ideology, as we have seen, is linked to Cartesianism. As such it runs counter to the Pascalian current, which also forms an important part of the Jansenist movement. The thought of Arnauld and Nicole thus cannot account for the entire movement. Lucien Goldmann's seminal research has shed much light on Jansenism's diverging currents by uncovering the importance of a rival faction headed by Barcos. In his analysis of Pascal in *Le Dieu caché* and in his edition of the *Correspondance de Martin de Barcos*, Goldmann demonstrates that Barcos was equal in stature to Arnauld and created an important opposing faction within the movement.[52]

That Barcos, a central figure in the Jansenist movement, should have been repressed from our historical consciousness[53] may probably be attributed to the extremist and subversive implications of his position. For Barcos, the world was so vitiated by original sin that he refused any complicity with it. Indeed, he altogether abandoned the quest for truth or justice in this world. Disparaging the mind and all human pretensions to knowledge as mired in sin, he preached absolute solitude.

Given that the Arnauldian faction believed in the efficacy of human reason and will to defend the true and the good in this world, Goldmann allies Pascal more with the Barcosian than with the Arnauldian faction. He argues that the grounds for the alliance between Pascal and Barcos lie in their rejection of this world. He quotes Besoigne's reference to Jansenism as "this little diversity of opinion between great theologians such as M. Arnauld, Nicole, La Lane, and others on the one hand, and M. Barcos and Pascal on the other."[54] Goldmann does, however, make a significant distinction between Pascal and Barcos: where Barcos gives an absolute *no* to this world, Pascal gives a paradoxical *yes* and *no*.

There is, however, another important link between Pascal and Barcos which Goldmann does not discuss. Both thinkers place the notion of original sin at the center of their epistemology. Sin results from the inversion or perversion of the ideal model that relates the individual to God and contaminates all modes of knowing. Original Sin occurred when the individual (specifically Adam) refused to regard God as his center and usurped God's central role. The consequence of this act has been a constant repetition of this inversion at other levels. The body became absorbed in its own concerns, thus highlighting its own presence and refusing to subordinate itself to the mind. Similarly, language took itself as its own center, thus widening the gap between itself and thought. By referring indirectly to itself, language figured itself. Self-reference is the very essence of sin. As Pascal writes, "everything tends toward itself: this is contrary to all order. . . . The bias toward self is the beginning of all disorder" ("tout tend à soi: cela est contre tout ordre. . . . la pente vers soi est le commencement de tout désordre" [S680, L421, B477]). The sinful self-reflexivity of the self, the body, and language are all experienced in their distance and exile from truth.

Whereas the Arnauldian current of Jansenism, under the influence of classicism, tries to overcome the obscurity created by its distance from truth, Barcos and Pascal put obscurity and distance at the center of their linguistic theory. An ideology of sin underlies this theory and develops a compatible aesthetic, one that is contrary to the Cartesian/Arnauldian one. The latter values the mind and correspondingly the mental side of the linguistic sign, the signified, over the body or the material aspect of the linguistic sign, the signifier. Barcos and Pascal reverse the Cartesian/Arnauldian priority by questioning the possibility of a pure thought that transcends the body of language. Moreover, they believe that to seek refuge in nostalgic fictions of transcending the materiality of language is to fall into the sin of pride. The presence of rhetorical figures, of carnal images, is necessary to remind us of our fallen state. In this Jansenist perspective, language has fallen from the semiological to the rhetorical realm where signs do not necessarily correspond to the world they claim to designate. Like classical ideology, however, Barcos and Pascal do ultimately subscribe to what Derrida calls a "Metaphysics of Presence." They long for a moment of original fullness when language and truth coincide, but they do not believe it can be brought about in this world through human efforts, as do classical theorists.

The Fall thus haunts Barcos's theory of knowledge and of language. The impenetrability of truth is owing to our relationship with death, the primary effect of the Fall: "This life is called the shadow of death because we are in continual darkness and obscurity where death threatens us and makes those who love God from the bottom of their hearts die with pain and chagrin."[55] Barcos's emphasis on the body, as opposed to the mind, stems from the connection of the body with death; death reminds us of the limitations of our true state which block direct access to a knowledge of God. Throughout his correspondence Barcos stresses the importance of a language that reflects the limitations of human knowledge. The only language possible is one that reflects back on its own mortality, which is expressed by the obscurity of veiled language.

As obscurity is essential to religious writing, according to Barcos, he defends Saint Paul's use of a rhetoric that obscures thought. Saint Paul's cultivation of obscurity through rhetorical expressions and linguistic games posed problems for translators, who asked whether they should correct the density and awkwardness of Saint Paul's language in order to clarify his discourse, or whether they should remain faithful to the seeming chaos of his text. It is "impossible to translate Saint Paul's Epistles because of his use of hyperboles, interrupted reasonings, imperfect comparisons, passages without continuity or order, many short and difficult expressions, without mentioning incongruities, mistakes against the rules of art and habit, and so many other things contrary to human sense."[56] The rough edges of Saint Paul's text, Barcos maintains, should not be smoothed out by the glossy rhetoric of a translation. Rather, the translation should strive to preserve the obscurity that is its essence.

The cultivation of obscurity, rooted in an epistemology that stresses human powerlessness, has a distinct polemical function: to humble humankind through a mortification of the mind.

> God wanted there to be more obscure places than transparent and intelligible ones in order to exercise the soul, thus showing that little knowledge suffices for their nourishment. But they have great need of being exercised in humility, punishment, mortification, and in all the virtues so as to gain eternal life by God's nourishment and the light of his word. . . . Thus it is not by making writing elegant, clear, and easy to understand by all kinds of people that souls are enlightened.[57]

Humility is humankind's recognition that it is not capable of attaining truth. Knowledge, then, must be acquired indirectly, through the emphasis on language's failure to represent. In fact, all understanding is locked in obscurity, a phenomenon that indirectly points to the Fall through the sense of inadequacy it brings about. To seek a direct knowledge, which is impossible, would be prideful; it would lead humans away from an appropriate assessment of their true state. To accept that all signs are obscure stimulates a self-reflection that will reveal the impotence of humans and render them humble.

Even if divine knowledge were somehow to become accessible, it would be destroyed the very moment that humans grasped it. Paradoxically, the ability of humans to comprehend divine language would undermine their comprehension, which needs a strong element of mystery at its center. Penetration is destruction; distancing is preservation. The very act of comprehending divine discourse is to destroy its authority. To penetrate this sacred secret would swell human pride. Religious discourse can hope to gain access to God only by keeping itself at a distance, so that a modicum of obscurity remains.

Although humans are shut off from truth because of the obscurity of language, this very obscurity forms another kind of truth, which is our distance from truth. The most truthful language is one that denounces any pretensions to truthfulness. It announces itself as false and underscores its distance from truth. Although Barcos did not explicitly say so, such a mode of communication is figurative. The primary relation between language and thought

is skewed by obscurity and thus gives rise to another relation, a
figurative one created by the inability of language to point clearly
to thought, which, in turn, becomes a new figure. Language figures
its own obscurity and the distance that separates language from
thought. A language that harps upon the obtrusive force of its figurative structure points to the Fall. But only Pascal fully developed
the way in which language, our primary instrument of knowledge,
has fallen from the semiological to the rhetorical sphere.

## PASCAL'S THEORY OF FIGURES: RHETORIC
## AS FALL AND AS REDEMPTION

Pascal develops a theory of figures based on obscurity which was
only implicit in Barcos. For Pascal, human language is obscure
and therefore always figures itself; it figures its own obscurity and
corruption. But language is not to be limited by its self-referential-
ity; it also has a figural reference beyond itself. This indirect or figural pointing to something beyond itself is complicated by its own
figural nature. The signifier can never enclose a single signified
or an indirect, figural signified; new, uncontrollable signifieds
may always slip past its guard. Yet precisely because language
is uncontrollably figurative, it opens up the possibility of slipping
past human meaning and of turning toward Redemption.

### The Judeo-Christian History

Pascal develops his theory of figures most explicitly in his discussion of the Jews and their relation to Christianity. In Pascal's
view, the Jewish religion laid the foundation for Christianity, and
the latter ultimately superseded the former. In what follows, I
show how the shift from Judaic law to the Christian vision is a
shift from a semiological to a figurative view of language. Like
classical discourse, Jewish discourse adopts a semiological system
that blinds itself to its fallen and figural nature. As a result, the
Jews fail to recognize the Messiah they predicted. Conversely,
Christian discourse accepts its fallen and figural nature which
enables Christians to recognize Jesus as the Messiah.

Pascal portrays the Jews as "the forerunners and heralds" ("les avant-coureurs et les hérauts" [S694, L454, B619]) who not only predicted the coming of the Messiah but also established the specific signs by which he would be recognized. As the "depository of the spiritual covenant," the Jews carry "for all to see the books foretelling the Messiah, assuring all nations that he must come in the manner foretold in the books they held open for all to read" ("à la vue de tout le monde ces livres qui prédisent leur Messie, assurant toutes les nations qu'il devait venir, et en la manière prédite dans les livres qu'ils tenaient ouverts à tout le monde" [S738, L502, B571; see also S9, L390, B617]). Their prophecies constitute semiological codes that enable one to interpret the signs of Christ as those of the true Messiah. One of these prophecies announces the downfall of Jewish law. The prophets said that "the law they had was only provisional, while they waited for the Messiah to give them his law" ("la loi qu'ils avaient n'était qu'en attendant celle du Messie" [S9, L390, B617; see also S718, L483, B726]). The Jewish prophets foresaw that Jewish law, a semiological system providing a literal, legalistic logic for the coding and decoding of signs, was only temporary; it would change after the coming of the Messiah. The new law of the Messiah would be figurative; as such, it would put in question the literal, Jewish law.

Although the Jews prophesied the end of their own law, Pascal says, they failed to understand what the prophecy meant. Similarly, although they transmitted the texts upon which divine truths were based, their law, their semiological codes, were not sufficient to interpret the texts properly. Because their interpretive codes operated along literal and not figurative lines, the Jews misunderstood their own texts and were blinded to the reality they designated. Imprisoned in the letter of their semiological system, "this carnal people" (S738, L502, B571) was attached only to "temporal goods" (S693, L453, B610), for they could not see the spiritual, figurative message. Pascal explains their literal reading of the world by pointing out that the Old Testament presents God as bestowing material benefits upon the Jewish people. He saved them from the Flood, he helped them cross the Red Sea, he led them into the promised land. Accustomed to God's material gifts, the Jews saw the Messiah as a Being who would also bestow mate-

rial goods upon them. They were thus unable to recognize the
divine personage of Christ, who appeared, not in material splendor
and wealth, but draped in rags. "The carnal Jews awaited a carnal
Messiah" (S318, L286, B609); the "carnal Jews understood neither the greatness nor the lowliness of the Messiah foretold in their
prophecies. They failed to recognize him in his greatness, . . .
they sought in him only a carnal greatness" ("Les Juifs charnels
n'entendaient ni la grandeur ni l'abaissement du Messie prédit
dans leurs prophéties. Ils l'ont méconnu dans sa grandeur prédite, . . . ils ne cherchaient en lui qu'une grandeur charnelle"
[S288, L256, B662]). The letter of Jewish law trapped them in a
hermeneutic circle. The law established the codes for the recognition of a truth they prophesied as lying outside their law. Their
understanding of this truth was, however, locked in by the literalness of their law, which did not allow them to recognize anything
that lay outside its codes.

To escape this hermeneutic impasse and to prove that Jesus
Christ is the Messiah, Pascal has to show that there is an alternative system, a figurative one, which transcends Jewish law. "For
if we believe that [the prophecies] have only one meaning, it is
certain that the Messiah has not come, but if they have two meanings, it is certain that he has come in Jesus Christ" ("Car si on
croit que [les prophéties] n'ont qu'un sens, il est sûr que le Messie
ne sera point venu, mais si elles ont deux sens il est sûr qu'il sera
venu en J-C" [S305, L274, B642]). Pascal seeks to demonstrate
that the prophecies have two meanings by showing that a figurative meaning was already implied in the Jewish literal, semiological system, although the Jews did not realize it. The Jewish people
"carry the books and love them and do not understand them"
("porte les livres et les aime et ne les entend point" [S736, L495,
B641]); they do not grasp the meaning of their own discourse,
which is figurative. Their semiological system allows for only one
literal meaning and is thus inadequate to decode its own signs.
Pascal uses this obstacle, the insufficiency of their semiological
system, to point to a new one.

Pascal transforms the Jews' misreading of their own texts into
a figure of the rhetorical nature of all language which he hopes
will ultimately point to God. In other words, he seeks to show that
Jewish discourse is already figurative; however, the Jews are un-

aware of it: they misread their own discourse. The Jews mistakenly believe that their texts point directly and clearly to the conditions that will enable them and others to recognize the Messiah. According to Pascal, however, their texts point only indirectly and obscurely to the Messiah. Pascal observes that, according to the Jews' prophecies in the Old Testament, the Messiah "will be rejected and will be the cause of scandal" ("sera rejeté et en scandale" [S738, L502, B571]), the prophets' law will be replaced by the Messiah's new law, and the obscurity of the prophets' discourse will prevent it from being properly understood. The prophets state that "their sayings are obscure and that their meaning will not be understood" (S737, L501, B659). In enunciating these conditions, the Jews intended them to designate a referent outside their semiological system. They believed that other people, not they, would misunderstand and reject the Messiah. After all, they felt that they wanted the Messiah and thus that, when he and his superior law appeared, they would abandon their own law. The literalness of Jewish law, however, limits the Jews to what its codes will allow them to perceive. As long as they hold to their law, they can never recognize the conditions that should lead them to abandon it. As the Messiah and his new law lie in a figurative system outside their semiological codes, they fail to recognize them. The Jews themselves thus necessarily fulfill the very conditions that their prophets had predicted, for they are the ones to reject the Messiah, misunderstand their own texts, and show the insufficiency of their own law. The Jews unintentionally figure themselves as cut off from God and imprisoned in language. Jewish discourse, then, is figural in spite of itself. And in referring back to its figural nature, it becomes the primary historical figure of a fallen discourse which does not recognize that it is fallen.

By pointing to its own fallenness, Jewish discourse points indirectly to what it misunderstands: the Messiah:

The Jews, by killing him in order not to accept him as the Messiah, conferred upon him the final sign that he was the Messiah.

Les Juifs en le tuant pour ne le point recevoir pour Messie, lui ont donné la dernière marque du Messie [S734, L488, B761].

> Those who rejected and crucified Jesus Christ, who was for them
> a cause of scandal, are also those who carry the books that bear wit-
> ness to him and say that he will be rejected and will be a cause
> of scandal. Thus they showed that he was the Messiah by refusing
> him.

> Ceux qui ont rejeté et crucifié Jésus-Christ qui leur a été en scan-
> dale sont ceux qui portent les livres qui témoignent de lui et qui
> disent qu'il sera rejeté et en scandale de sorte qu'ils ont marqué
> que c'était lui en le refusant [S738, L502, B571].

In their very inability to recognize the Messiah, the Jews indirectly
point to him. Paradoxically, the fallen nature of Jewish discourse
figures Christ, the Redeemer. The Jews, blind to the fallen and
figural nature of their own discourse, blindly serve as figures of
the Christian new order, which subverts the codes in which they
believe.

The Jews' very inability to recognize that their codes are already
figurative becomes a figure of their status as figure. Blindness or
obscurity is an important part of the figurative structure. Figures
are created by a strange mixture of clarity, which facilitates representation, and obscurity, which impedes direct representation but
creates an indirect reference. "Nature has perfections to show
that it is the image of God and has imperfections to show that it
is no more than his image" ("La nature a des perfections pour
montrer qu'elle est l'image de Dieu et des défauts pour montrer
qu'elle n'en est que l'image" [S762, L934, B580]). Nature, in this
instance, functions as a figure of God because it fulfills two essential conditions: similarity and difference or, in other terms, clarity
and obscurity. Because nature manifests some perfection, partici-
pating in a part of God's perfection, it is able to establish a link
with God. If there were no basis for association, be it natural or
conventional, nature would be powerless to evoke God. If, however, the similarities were to coincide, or overlap significantly,
nature would be so powerful that it could replace God. Nature
would cease to serve as a representation and would become an
end in itself. To counteract the similarities, Pascal explains, God
added important differences which can be created by obscurity.
Differences point to the sign's impotence. Through the obscurity

of difference, nature points to the defects that distance its signs from God by preventing any confusion between its signs and their objects. Difference and obscurity, then, are not defects that inhibit the signification process; rather, they enhance it. Because the sign does not fuse with the object, it creates a figure that brings out its fallen status as figure.

The Jews, in their capacity as figures, function in ways similar to that of nature viewed as figure.

> Figurative.
> Nothing is so much like charity as cupidity, and nothing is so unlike it. Thus the Jews, rich with possessions to flatter their greed, were very much like Christians and very much unlike them. And thus they had the two qualities they had to have: they were very much like the Messiah in order to figure him, and were very much unlike him so that they would not be suspect as witnesses.

> Figuratif.
> Rien n'est si semblable à la charité que la cupidité et rien n'est si contraire. Ainsi les juifs pleins de biens qui flattaient leur cupidité, étaient très conformes aux Chrétiens et très contraires. Et par ce moyen ils avaient les deux qualités qu'il fallait qu'ils eussent d'être très conformes au Messie, pour le figurer, et très contraires pour n'être point témoins suspects [S508, L615, B663].

The Jews are made to function as figures and establish the conditions necessary for the functioning of all figures: similarity and difference. Like the Messiah, the Jews possess many admirable qualities that evoke him and make them worthy of him. They are a people of "diligence, faithfulness, extraordinary zeal and are known to all the world. . . . So here are the people of the world the least susceptible to the suspicion of favoring us. They are the most strict and zealous for their law and prophets, who carry their books without corruption" ("une diligence et fidélité et d'un zèle extraordinaire et connues de toute la terre. . . . De sorte que voilà le peuple du monde le moins suspect de nous favoriser et le plus exact et zélé qui se puisse dire pour sa loi et pour ses prophètes, qui porte [leurs livres] incorrompus" [S738, L502, B571]). Their dissimilarity lies in their blindness to their own figural nature, which is a crucial part of their function as figure. "If

the Jews had all been converted by Christ we would have left
only suspect witnesses" ("Si les Juifs eussent été tous convertis
par Jésus-Christ nous n'aurions plus que des témoins suspects"
[S492, L592, B750]). By failing to penetrate the veil of obscurity
or even to perceive that there is a veil, the Jews lend credence to
those who do penetrate it. Their blindness gives credibility to
those who properly interpreted Christ's signs.

Figures function when obscurity puts clarity in question:

> A portrait conveys absence and presence, pleasantness and un-
> pleasantness. Reality excludes absence and unpleasantness.
> *Figures.* To know whether the law and the sacrifices are literal
> or figurative, we must see whether the prophets in speaking of
> these things thought and looked no further, so that they saw only
> the old covenant, or whether they saw something else of which it
> was the representation, for in a portrait we see the thing figured.

> Un portrait porte absence et présence, plaisir et déplaisir. La
> réalité exclut absence et déplaisir.
> *Figures.* Pour savoir si la loi et les sacrifices sont réalité ou figure
> il faut voir si les prophètes en parlant de ces choses y arrêtaient
> leur vue et leur pensée, en sorte qu'ils n'y vissent que cette ancienne
> alliance, ou s'ils y voient quelque autre chose dont elle fut la pein-
> ture. Car dans un portrait on voit la chose figurée [S291, L260,
> B678].

The portrait, cited as an example of a figure, has two dimensions,
presence and absence, whereas reality operates on only one dimension: presence.[58] A portrait contains presence for it can introduce
"the thing figured" as if it were present by acting as a substitute
for the represented object. It is, however, only a substitute, and
it must not be confused with the object itself. In this connection
the image of the portrait is revealing, for it underlines the material
aspect of the representative element as a figure of something else.
By insisting on the figurative element of the representing sign, it
is made distinct from the represented object. Were they to be
confused, the portrait would lose its status as a figure capable of
representing something outside itself. It is precisely its absence of
reality which maintains the portrait in its role as figure. This
absence is crucial: were it not perceived, one might be tempted

to confuse the figure with reality, for reality has no absence at all. Absence is a necessary defect that permits the correct functioning of any representative system.

Because God, too, is partly present, partly absent, figures may be the only means of access to the divine. "*Figures*. . . . Because the things of God are inexpressible, they cannot be spoken of otherwise" (*"Figures*. . . . Car les choses de Dieu étant inexprimables, elles ne peuvent être dites autrement" [S303, L272, B687]). God and figures share a similar structure: a play of presence and absence, clarity and obscurity. "It is . . . useful for us that God is partly hidden and partly revealed, as it is equally dangerous for man to know God without knowing his own wretchedness as to know his wretchedness without knowing God" ("Il est . . . utile pour nous que Dieu soit caché en partie, et découvert en partie, puisqu'il est également dangereux à l'homme de connaître Dieu sans connaître sa misère, et de connaître sa misère sans connaître Dieu" [S690, L446, B586]). "What is seen on earth indicates neither a total exclusion nor a manifest presence of divinity, but the presence of a God who hides himself. Everything bears this character" ("Ce qui y paraît ne marque ni une exclusion totale, ni une présence manifeste de divinité, mais la présence d'un Dieu qui se cache. Tout porte ce caractère" [S690, L449, B556]).

Pascal's rhetorical system, viewed from the perspective of faith, tries to be all-inclusive. No matter which way the figures turn, if followed out to their end, they ultimately should figure the same truths: "There is nothing on earth which does not show either man's wretchedness or God's mercy, either man's helplessness without God or man's strength with God" ("Il n'y a rien sur la terre qui ne montre ou la misère de l'homme ou la miséricorde de Dieu, ou l'impuissance de l'homme sans Dieu ou la puissance de l'homme avec Dieu" [S705, L468, B562]). Figures, even when they do not point directly to God, may do so indirectly in the Pascalian perspective of faith. The Jews' blindness establishes the centrality of obscurity which Pascal transforms into a figure of figural truth: "Recognize then the truth of religion in its very obscurity" ("Reconnaissez donc la vérité de la religion dans l'obscurité même de la religion" [S690, L439, B565]). The ability of words to escape their denotative role and to create new, perhaps unintended, meanings points to their figurative function. And this slippery property of figures becomes a figure of figurative, fallen language. The obscurity of figures can point not only back to itself but also to the corruption of humankind: "What are we to conclude from all our obscurities if not our unworthiness?" ("Que conclurons-nous de toutes nos obscurités, sinon notre indignité?" [S690, L445, B558]; "S'il n'y avait point d'obscurité, l'homme ne sentirait point sa corruption" [S690, L446, B586]). And the corruption of fallen language can figure Jesus Christ, the ultimate figure of God. As both man and God, Jesus Christ, who is aware that he represents both absence and presence, Jewishness and non-Jewishness, satisfies the conditions necessary for discourse in a fallen world that is aware of having fallen into figures.

Many of Pascal's fragments suggest that he has already made the wager that there is a God who, by definition, transcends rhetoric.[59] These fragments, written from a perspective of faith, reveal that, for Pascal, divine discourse is devoid of slippery figures and constitutes an unfallen linguistic model. The Cartesian and classical ideal of the total coincidence of language with thought is possible, according to Pascal, but only in God, a Being situated outside the fallen world: "In God, word and intention do not differ, for he is truthful; nor do word and effect differ, for he is powerful; nor do means and effect differ, for he is wise" ("En Dieu la parole ne diffère pas de l'intention car il est véritable, ni la parole de l'effet car il est puissant, ni les moyens de l'effet car il est sage" [S416, L968, B654]). Jesus Christ, speaking from a state of grace, can also communicate with perfect clarity:

> *Proofs of Jesus Christ.*—Jesus Christ said great things so simply that he seems not have thought them, and yet so clearly that it is obvious that he thought them. This clarity coupled with this simplicity is admirable.

> *Preuves de Jésus-Christ.*—Jésus-Christ a dit les choses grandes si simplement qu'il semble qu'il ne les a pas pensées, et si nettement néanmoins qu'on voit bien ce qu'il en pensait. Cette clarté jointe à cette naïveté est admirable [S340, L309, B797].

This linguistic ideal was accessible to humans only through their connection with God in their prelapsarian state and can be realized only through Redemption.

In the *Pensées,* humankind's relationship to a nonfigural, divine discourse structures both the idyllic prefallen state and the post-fallen world. Pascal characterizes the prelapsarian state as one in which humans and God shared a common sign system; they were in clear and direct communication with each other. In fact, in the only prosopopeia created by Pascal, God communicates directly with humankind: "But you are no longer in the state in which I formed you. I created man holy, innocent, perfect. I filled him with light and intelligence, I communicated to him my glory and my wonders. Man's eye then beheld the majesty of God. He was not then in the darkness that now blinds his sight, nor was he subject to mortality and the woes that afflict him" ("Mais vous n'êtes plus maintenant en l'état où je vous ai formés. J'ai créé l'homme saint, innocent, parfait, je l'ai rempli de lumière et d'intelligence, je lui ai communiqué ma gloire et mes merveilles. L'oeil de l'homme voyait alors la majesté de Dieu. Il n'était pas alors dans les ténèbres qui l'aveuglent, ni dans la mortalité et dans les misères qui l'affligent" [S182, L149, B430]). In their prelapsarian state humans were bathed in light, removed from obscurity and blindness, and thus they had no need for figures, which in fact could not function in a world of direct intelligence.

After the Fall, God not only withdrew from the world but also removed most of his light and the signs of his existence: " . . . man is fallen from a state of glory and communication with God" (" . . . l'homme est déchu d'un état de gloire et de communication avec Dieu" [S313, L281, B613]). God no longer appears to speak to humans: "The eternal silence of these infinite spaces terrifies me" ("Le silence éternel de ces espaces infinis m'effraie" [S233, L201, B206]). Whereas one had come to expect the indications of divine guidance, one now finds only a deafening silence: "the universe [is] mute" [S229, L198, B693]. Pascal suggests that God does still speak to humans, but he does so in a language that is not immediately accessible to human sign systems. After the Fall, there can be no semiological code that can join humans to God. For Pascal, a semiological, classical discourse can exist only in an ideal state before the Fall. Adam had the power sought by Descartes; he was granted mastery over the earth within the order of creation by his God-given gift of naming the animals in Eden (Gen. 2:19). And God, who endorsed his choice, guaranteed the correspondence between word and thing named. The evocation of this ideal world serves to accentuate the fall into rhetoric. Rhetoric is the heritage of the Fall.

For Pascal, the attempt of classicists and Cartesians to transcend rhetoric, or at least to subordinate it to their semiological structures, is the ultimate act of pride. They and their discourses are fallen, yet, like the Jews, they are blinded to it. Their texts, like Jewish texts, are figures of an unintended meaning. Although the classical, Cartesian, and Jewish discourses believe themselves to be guided by a logic and law that can control the production and interpretation of meaning, Pascal shows that these discourses produce unintended meanings and are inhabited by a rhetoric that puts their semiological system in question. Their blindness to their fallen and figural nature becomes a figure of all rational consciousness which will always be blinded to its own texts. All logical systems may be unaware of the direction in which they are headed. And, of course, Pascal's text is no exception. Although rhetoric may wreak havoc with logic, it shows that language can express meaning indirectly. In this way, rhetoric opens itself up to a Christian discourse that, in this fallen world, can communicate only indirectly.

Although the Christians, unlike the Jews, know that their language is fallen and figural, they are unable to interpret the figures with any certainty. Pascal bemoans the fact that there are no new miracles to indicate that our interpretations are right or wrong. In this fallen world, Christian discourse, like Jewish discourse, may be blinded to the unpredictable turns of its own figures. Indeed, it may be impossible to know with certainty whether figures only turn understanding back toward their own linguistic structure, or whether they figure something outside their structure, either God, or perhaps something other. Pascal's theory of figures contains the seeds of its own possible destruction. Lacking certainty, all one can do is wager that language's figures of its own otherness will turn toward God's Otherness.

# 2

# The Fall from Truth into Language

"Everything arrived through figures" ("Tout arrivait en figures" [S299, L268, B683]). As discussed in chapter 1, figures, by producing incompatible meanings, remind us that we are cut off from an absolute truth. They put in question the semiological codes that give the impression of a transcendent truth. Indeed, for Pascal, the Christian religion is based on the notion of a hidden God who hides his truth from human signs: "men are in darkness and removed from God, . . . he has hidden himself from their knowledge, . . . this is even the very name he gives himself in the Scriptures, *Deus absconditus*" ("les hommes sont dans les ténèbres et dans l'éloignement de Dieu, . . . il s'est caché à leur connaissance, . . . c'est même le nom qu'il se donne dans les Ecritures, *Deus absconditus*" [S681, L427, B194]). Although God did establish some signs of his existence, he covered them up, enshrouding them in obscurity. Severed from certain knowledge of a transcendent truth, humans have fallen into a world of opaque signs: "I look everywhere and all I see is darkness. Nature offers me nothing that does not give rise to doubt and anxiety" ("Je regarde de toutes parts, et je ne vois partout qu'obscurité. La nature ne m'offre rien qui ne soit matière de doute et d'inquiétude" [S682, L429, B229]). This epistemological fall from truth into language generates an aporia. From the perspective of uncertainty, one side of the aporia, figural language is the only certain reality. It places humans in a position where they cannot locate with certainty a truth outside its

41

linguistic bounds. But from the perspective of faith, the other side of the aporia, the epistemological fall itself becomes a figure of our fallen state: God has punished humans for their sin by imprisoning them within discourse.

In this chapter I want to show how the *Pensées*, viewed from the perspective of faith, dramatize the fall from truth into language. The drama presupposes that the narrator, whom I assume corresponds to a part of Pascal, has transcended language to acquire, through faith, the certainty of belief in God. This supposition situates Pascal outside the text for, as master of his language, he uses it to manipulate his readers. Such a view is consonant with the traditional reading of the *Pensées'* rhetoric.[1] Although this reading can be justified by the *Pensées*, it does not account for all the Pascalian text in which other "Pascals" speak from other perspectives. In this chapter, therefore, I examine the relationship between the perspective of faith and its opposite, the perspective of uncertainty, where the narrator is trapped within language.

## THE HERMENEUTIC CIRCLE OF LANGUAGE

In the *Pensées*, Pascal explores the problematic relationship between truth and its representation in a fallen world. In order to punish our sins, God has withdrawn his presence as a guarantor of truth, and thus we are in a world where we have fallen away from any certain knowledge of truth. At first glance Pascal's statement—"The figure was modeled upon the truth. And the truth was recognized from the figure" ("La figure a été faite sur la vérité. Et la vérité a été reconnue sur la figure" [S667, L826, B673])—might seem to contradict itself. The first clause suggests that truth is outside of and prior to the figure, whereas the second one implies the reverse: the figure is anterior to truth, for the truth can be recognized only by a correspondence to a preceding figure. The *Pensées* strongly advise that one should take such contradictions seriously: " . . . to understand an author's meaning, all contradictory passages must be reconciled. . . . Every author has a meaning that reconciles all contradictory passages, or else he has no meaning at all" (" . . . pour entendre le sens d'un auteur il faut accorder tous les passages contraires. . . . Tout auteur a un sens auquel tous les passages contraires s'accordent ou il n'a point de sens du tout" [S289, L257, B684]). From a perspective of faith and only from that perspective, as I show, can there be a point of view from which these clauses can be reconciled.

In this fragment the narrator is describing the hermeneutic circle in which all human attempts at knowledge are trapped. Since the Fall, all representations of truth depend on a prior knowledge of that truth. Yet our access to that truth must necessarily be mediated through human forms. These forms set up the criteria for truth, which are not transmitted to us by any means outside our representations. Therefore it is our representations that establish the basis for our ability to perceive truth as truth. In this perspective, then, the representation is both posterior and anterior to the truth. All human efforts to arrive at solid and certain truth fall into language that is structured by the hermeneutic circle.[2]

This circular structure is echoed throughout the *Pensées*. The narrator describes the impossibility of arriving at a comprehensive understanding of the world: "Thus since all things are both caused and causing, assisted and assisting, mediate and immediate, and all is held together by a natural and imperceptible chain which binds together things most distant and most different, I maintain that it is equally impossible to know the parts without knowing the whole as to know the whole without knowing the individual parts" ("Donc toutes choses étant causées et causantes, aidées et aidantes, médiates et immédiates, et toutes s'entretenant par un lien naturel et insensible qui lie les plus éloignées et les plus différentes, je tiens impossible de connaître les parties sans connaître le tout, non plus que de connaître le tout sans connaître particulièrement les parties" [S230, L199, B72]). The narrator also presents several other variations on this hermeneutic trap: "Our minds and feelings are formed by the company we keep; our minds and feelings are ruined by the company we keep. Thus good or bad company respectively improves or corrupts them. It is therefore very important to make the right choice so that we improve rather than corrupt them. And we cannot make this choice unless we have already improved and not corrupted our judgment. We are thus caught in a vicious circle, from which those who escape are most fortunate" ("On se forme l'esprit et le sentiment par les conversations, on se gâte l'esprit et le sentiment par les conversations. Ainsi les bonnes ou les mauvaises le forment ou le gâtent. Il importe donc de tout de bien savoir choisir pour se le former et ne le point gâter. Et on ne peut faire ce choix si on ne l'a déjà formé et point gâté. Ainsi cela fait un cercle dont sont bienheureux ceux qui sortent" [S658, L814, B6; see also S454, L527, B40]).

The dilemmas that the narrator articulates here are fundamental, and they underlie the *Pensées* as a whole. They force us to ask whether one can escape to an origin, a point outside the hermeneutic circle, which will ground our understanding of truth. Pascal recognizes that knowledge requires the existence of a preceding model which confers meaning upon new phenomena by assigning them appropriate coordinates within the structure of the whole. Can isolated, radically new phenomena be perceived and understood if there is no epistemological paradigm into which they can be integrated? This prerequisite for knowledge raises one of the most basic questions posed by philosophy: How is a first knowledge possible if it must be based on preexisting knowledge? How is the first paradigm established? This dilemma is what drove Plato to his famous doctrine that all knowledge is recollection. In the *Meno*, Plato has Socrates say: "the truth of things is always in the soul . . . since [the soul] has seen all things, both in this world and in the other, there is nothing it has not learnt . . . so there is nothing to prevent one who has recollected—learnt, as we call it—one single thing from discovering all the rest for himself . . . seeking or learning is nothing but recollection."[3] According to Plato, knowledge is acquired, not through the senses or through reason, but through recollection in this life of truths seen and known by the soul before its incarnation.[4]

Pascal, like Saint Augustine,[5] feels a strong affinity with Plato and uses Platonic notions as a basis for certain Christian doctrines: "Plato, to dispose people toward Christianity" ("Platon, pour disposer au christianisme" [S505, L612, B219]). Pascal's solution to the above dilemma, when he speaks from the perspective of faith, bears a strong resemblance to the Platonic doctrine of recollection. Pascal develops a Christian notion of recollection and of an original pre-Fall vision of the whole in connection with his doctrine of the three orders,[6] which provides an escape from the hermeneutic circle. According to this doctrine, humans had already experienced this fundamental knowledge when they were in their

original, prefallen state. Although they have almost entirely forgotten this state, a present intuition of the former knowledge
remains, allowing them to remember it and serving as a foundation
for their systems of knowledge. Pascal argues that all knowledge
since the Fall may be understood in relation to three distinct orders
of being: the body, the mind, and grace (charity or the will). Pascal
articulates his doctrine:

> The lust of the flesh, the lust of the eyes, pride, and so on. There
> are three orders of things: flesh, spirit, and will. The carnal are rich
> men and kings. Their interest is in the body. The interest of inquir-
> ers and scientists is in the mind. The interest of the wise is in justice.
> God should govern everything and everything should be related to
> him. In things of the flesh, lust reigns supreme; in things of the
> mind, curiosity; in wisdom, pride.

> Concupiscence de la chair, concupiscence des yeux, orgueil, etc.
> Il y a trois ordres de choses. La chair, l'esprit, la volonté. Les char-
> nels sont les riches, les rois. Ils ont pour objet le corps. Les curieux
> et savants, ils ont pour objet l'esprit. Les sages, ils ont pour objet
> la justice. Dieu doit régner sur tout et tout se rapporter à lui. Dans
> les choses de la chair règne proprement sa concupiscence. Dans
> les spirituels, la curiosité proprement. Dans la sagesse l'orgueil
> proprement [S761, L933, B460; see also S339, L308, B793].

The notion that understanding has different levels of being has
a philosophic history; its classical exposition is Plato's theory of
the divided line in Book VII of the *Republic*.[7] Plato maintains a
fourfold distinction of orders of knowledge. His discussion of the
imagination (*eikasia*) and of sensation (*pistis*) corresponds to the
Pascalian first order of the body; Plato's analysis of thought
(*dianoia*) relates to the Pascalian second order of the mind; and
his notion of intellection (*noesis*), a recollection of ideas existing
outside images, evokes the Pascalian third order of grace. Such
categories of being are commonplace in Christian writing and
may be found in Saint Paul, Saint Augustine, Sebond, Charron,
and Bérulle.

In Pascal's doctrine of the three orders, those enclosed in the
first order of the body, the Jews, for example, perceive only the
most literal level of things and are blinded to figurative meaning.

Those confined to the second order of the mind understand a figurative meaning that is perceived by the mind. As long as one is
limited to one of these two orders, one is locked within the hermeneutic circle. Knowledge perceived through either the sense data
of the body or the symbolic dimension of the mind is trapped
within the circular relation of truth to representation. Only from
the perspective of faith is there a way out, according to Pascal.
The key lies in the third order of grace, which establishes a pre-Fall
epistemological model. On occasion the third order transmits
what is variously called an instinct, a sentiment, a natural light,
"an inward disposition completely holy" ("une disposition intérieure toute sainte" [S413, L381, B286]), which enables us to
remember our prefallen wisdom. According to Pascal, who speaks
from the perspective of faith, the recollection of this knowledge
escapes the mediating forms of representation associated with the
mind or the body. Emanating from the third order of grace, this
knowledge transcends the hermeneutic circle. By furnishing an
absolute perspective, the third order grounds and interprets the
perceptions of the first two levels.

The knowledge from the third order, however, is sometimes difficult to decipher, for it is not perceived through or communicated
by the institutionalized languages and forms to which we are
accustomed. It comes to us through what Pascal calls the heart:
an instinct, a feeling, an intuition, an interior light. By being
aware of the feelings that help to recollect the prelapsarian state,
humans become conscious of a connection with their origins, the
foundation of all knowledge. "That is the state in which men are
today. They retain some feeble instinct from the happiness of
their first nature" ("Voilà l'état où les hommes sont aujourd'hui.
Il leur reste quelque instinct impuissant du bonheur de leur première nature" [S182, L149, B430]). Light from the third order,
although faint, does penetrate human consciousness, and "barely
does there remain a glimmer of its author" ("à peine lui reste-t-il
une lumière confuse de son auteur" [S182, L149, B430]). By heed-
ing the signals emanating from this light, humans can "become
exalted through their inner feeling that remains from their past
greatness" ("s'élever dans le sentiment intérieur qui leur reste de
leur grandeur passée [S240, L208, B435]). Through the heart's
capacity for recollection humans are linked to their original per-

fection and wisdom; thus they are given a basis for the knowledge that lifts them—if only occasionally and imperfectly—out of the hermeneutic circle.

In light of these points, one can now see how Pascal, at least from the perspective of faith, resolves the seeming contradiction in the fragment cited at the beginning of this section. The first part of the fragment ("The figure was modeled upon the truth"), spoken from the perspective of the third order of grace, establishes a model of the truth-representation relationship. In the third order, truth is unveiled and exists independently of the mediating forms of language. Moreover, from this perspective representation is sufficient to capture truth. Such an equivalence between truth and its representation defines the unfallen world; it posits an epistemological ideal against which the second phrase is measured and found wanting. The second part of this fragment ("the truth was recognized from the figure") must inevitably fall short of the ideal because it is spoken from the only perspective available to humans, a fallen one belonging to the first and second orders. From this perspective, our access to absolute truth is mediated by our signifying system which is trapped in the hermeneutic circle. From this limited perspective, it appears as though we are cut off from any direct contact with truth; human language here must create the forms of truth rather than discover them in a higher order, and it can never be certain that its representations coincide with truth.

By shifting the perspective of grace to a human perspective, the fragment dramatizes humankind's fall from truth into language. It is thus crucial to understanding the *Pensées,* for it expresses Pascal's primary model of an epistemological fall. It clearly establishes that we cannot discuss the *Pensées* in terms of epistemologies, but only in terms of language which determines our notions of truthfulness.

According to Pascal, the only way to transcend the hermeneutic circle of language and our fallen nature is first to dig ourselves deeper into a consciousness of the corruption of language that imprisons us. The narrator uses the discourses appropriate to the first and second orders of body and mind to help his readers understand that they are indeed fallen out of truth into language.[8] Meeting them on their own grounds, he first adopts their discourses and then shows them to be trapped within language and cut off from truth. He then turns around the whole interpretive framework and transforms the very consciousness that we are imprisoned in language into the means which may make it possible for us to escape it and know the truth. The insight that we are locked within discourse—in particular, the discourses of the first and second orders—is a sign of another kind of truth, the truth of our fallen condition: "we must use the very locus where we fell in order to rise from our fall" ("il faut que nous nous servions du lieu même où nous sommes tombés pour nous relever de notre chute").[9]

The hermeneutic circle thus functions as a pivotal point in Pascal's rhetoric of persuasion because, although it is a secular structure suggesting our epistemologically fallen state, it also operates as an allegory of the religious structure that indicates our historically fallen state of sin. Both structures make humans realize that they are imprisoned within their particular network of images which blocks access to a transcendent truth: "For, as our sins keep us enveloped in corporal and earthly things, they are not only the punishment for our sins, but also they provide the opportunity to commit yet new ones and they are the cause of the first ones" ("Car, comme nos péchés nous retiennent enveloppés parmi les choses corporelles et terrestres, et qu'elles ne sont pas seulement la peine de nos péchés, mais encore l'occasion d'en faire de nouveaux et la cause des premiers").[10] Pascal's characterization of sin evokes the impasse created by the hermeneutic circle: "We should think of ourselves as criminals kept in a prison filled with images of their savior" ("Nous devons nous considérer comme des criminels dans une prison toute remplie des images de leur libérateur").[11]

Only Christianity provides an escape, for sin implies the possibility of salvation as well as of damnation. After showing the readers that they are trapped in language's hermeneutic circle and that their captivity represents a fall, Pascal then encourages them to shift away from the dead-end secular structure of the hermeneutic circle toward the more open-ended religious structure as defined by the third order. Once within the discursive world of the first and second orders structured by the hermeneutic circle, it is important to leap into the third order.[12] The *Pensées* invite this leap by showing how the first two orders are trapped in language and how they continually undercut themselves.

## DISCOURSES OF THE SECOND ORDER
## OF THE MIND

A discussion of the three orders would normally proceed in a sequential fashion—first, second, third (body, mind, God), or the reverse—presumably reflecting a proper hierarchical structure. I have chosen instead to analyze them out of sequence, starting with the second order and then shifting to the first one. I make references to the third order but do not treat it fully, as I do the others, for one cannot, according to Pascal, treat the third order rationally. (It would indeed be prideful to believe that one can know that order as well as the other two.) The traditional sequential ordering corresponds to the Platonic and Cartesian hierarchy that privileges the mind over the body. However, this hierarchy does not accord with the way Pascal's text functions. Pascal puts in question the traditional power accorded the discourse of the mind through the discourse of the body. The reversal of orders corresponds to the model established by the fragment: "The figure was modeled upon the truth. And the truth was recognized from the figure." The first part evokes the traditional belief that the discourse of the mind can capture truth through its forms of representation; the second part questions this ideal and suggests that truth is created by our linguistic forms. The discourse of the body thus makes us aware that we have fallen into the body of language, that is, into formal semiological codes that determine thought. The first order's discourse of the body demystifies the pretensions of the second order's discourse of the mind to arrive at a transcendent truth. The demystification is of course brought about by reason, the second order. But reason can understand itself only by realizing that it is caught in arbitrary, semiological codes of the first order of the body. It is only when reason realizes how it is a function of language that it can hope, through language, to point to something beyond itself, namely God.

## The Discourse of Successiveness and Sin

Pascal defines his discourse of reason against the background of Cartesian rational discourse. The latter seeks to found secular truths outside the hermeneutic circle; the former seeks to undermine such truths by reinscribing them within language's hermeneutic circle. Both discourses focus on the problem of the successive ordering of parts and its relation to knowledge.[13] Cartesian reason presupposes a logical ordering of parts that will add up to a whole. In his *Discourse on Method,* Descartes presents four rules, one of which is to divide problems into as many parts as is necessary to resolve them; another is to "conduct my thoughts in an orderly way, beginning with the simplest objects and the easiest to know, in order to climb gradually, as by degrees, as far as the knowledge of the most complex, and even supposing some order among those objects which do not precede each other naturally."[14] These "long chains of reasonings" gave Descartes the idea that if "one always keeps the right order for one thing to be deduced from that which precedes it, there can be nothing so distant that one does not reach it eventually, or so hidden that one cannot discover it."[15] For Descartes, then, the ordering of elements into long chains of reason is the means of arriving at truth.

In opposition to Descartes, Pascal believes that the ordering of elements into chains of reason of any length merely creates the illusion of wholeness and unity leading to knowledge. For Pascal, although the ordering of parts must form successive chains, the chains extend infinitely such that they cannot be encompassed by a whole. Successiveness, despite its traditional link with unity and order, actually creates disunity and ultimately undermines order, suggesting our distance from truth or origin. Order presupposes that one arranges the parts in a sequence that takes place over time. But the parts, if spread out over time, cannot be grasped as a whole. They can be seized only as fragmented segments that appear in succession, each one at an even longer distance from the origin. In the infinite universe, the chains of reason may be so long and intricate that only partial glimpses are available at any given moment. Yet if the discourse of reason, seeking to counteract the effects of the infinite, reduces the infinitely complex parts to a single, abstract model, it will necessarily exclude important details. Its apprehension of the world will always be partial.

For Pascal, all reason is successive and successiveness is the result and experience of the Fall:

> Six days to create one, six ages to create the other. The six days that Moses represents for the creation of Adam are only an image for creating Christ and the church. If Adam had not sinned and Jesus Christ had not come, there would have been only one covenant and one age of man, and the creation would have been represented as accomplished at one single moment.

> Les six jours pour former l'un, les six âges pour former l'autre. Les six jours que Moïse représente pour la formation d'Adam ne sont que la peinture des six âges pour former Jésus-Christ et l'église. Si Adam n'eût point péché et que Jésus-Christ ne fût point venu il n'y eût eu qu'une seule alliance, qu'un seul âge des hommes et la création eût été représentée comme faite en un seul temps [S489, L590, B656].

What is striking about this vision of a nonfallen world is the absence of time. A nonfallen world would have been created all at once and would have been characterized by only one age. Unity and instantaneity, as marks of a nonfallen world, evoke a model of an ideal world against which the present one is measured. The present world falls short of the ideal; it is pictured as being divided into successive ages, and the creation is represented as taking place on successive days. Had Adam not sinned, there would be only one age and the creation would have been represented as occurring all at once. Successivity, then, indicates our sinful state.

In his unfinished essay, "On the Geometric Mind," Pascal shows how successiveness undercuts the reasoning process. First he gives a model of rational clarity and truth. According to his model, no word should be used unless its meaning has already been explained; no proposition should be advanced unless it has been demonstrated by previously known truths. Such a method, however, is impossible, as Pascal admits, because it is limited by reason which is incapable of arriving at a first truth, for propositions about first truths always presuppose other propositions, and so on ad infinitum:

> . . . it is evident that the first terms that one would like to define would presuppose others to explain them and that, in the same

way, the first propositions that one would like to prove would presuppose others that would precede them; thus it is clear that we
would never arrive at the first ones.

> . . . il est évident que les premiers termes qu'on voudrait définir,
> en supposerait de précédents pour servir à leur explication, et que
> de même les premières propositions qu'on voudrait prouver en sup-
> poserait d'autres qui les précédassent; et ainsi il est clair qu'on
> n'arriverait jamais aux premières.[16]

Reason seeks absolute clarity through the successiveness of its definitions and proofs, but the successiveness reaches no end; it simply
stretches itself out infinitely so that it cannot be grasped as a whole.

All one has, then, is pure successiveness, with neither origin
nor end. Successiveness thus cannot provide a rational order because it is trapped within the hermeneutic circle. Unable to arrive
at an immediate, direct grasp of things, one cannot apprehend elements of the second order in themselves but must have them explained in terms of something that is other. Each term must be
elucidated through its relation to other terms; each proposition
should be clarified by its reference to other propositions. Rational
knowledge requires the establishment of a chain or a connecting
thread ordering all the links or parts so that every new word or
proposition builds on what has already been established. This
chain, however, will lead us around in circles, for there is no term
or proposition that stands free to serve as a foundation for all the
rest. Reason is thus caught in the hermeneutic circle.

Many of reason's attempts to escape the hermeneutic circle
through what may appear to be messages transmitted from the
third order turn out to be illusory—rational fictions of the mind.
The rational structures of language spin around in circles and
cannot arrive at a fixed meaning based on their own givens. For-
tunately, they have received a supplement from nature which communicates without words:

> We see that some words cannot be defined; if nature had not
> made up for this flaw by providing a common idea to all men, all
> our expressions would be confused; but we do use them with assur-

ance and certainty as if they were explained in a perfectly clear
fashion because nature herself gave us, *without the use of language,*
clearer intelligence than the one we could acquire through our
explanations.

> On voit assez de là qu'il y a des mots incapables d'être définis;
> et si la nature n'avait supplée à ce défaut par une idée pareille
> qu'elle a donnée à tous les hommes, toutes nos expressions seraient
> confuses; au lieu qu'on en use avec la même assurance et la même
> certitude que s'ils étaient expliqués d'une manière exempte
> d'équivoques; parce que la nature nous en a elle-même donné, *sans
> paroles* une intelligence plus nette que celle que l'art nous acquiert
> par nos explications [emphasis added].[17]

The geometrical order assumes that it is only through our natural light ("lumière naturelle") that human understanding has a
solid foundation. Human understanding is true only to the extent
that "the natural order guarantees it instead of language" ("la
nature le soutenant au défaut du discours").[18] The origin of this
"natural light," however, is ambiguous. Pascal's essay suggests
that it may come from the third order. If so, it would be possible
to transcend the hermeneutic circle. The "natural light" provides
stable points of reference; it transmits "primitive words that are
not subject to definition, and principles so clear that none clearer
can be found to prove them" ("des mots primitifs qu'on ne peut
plus définir, et . . . des principes si clairs qu'on n'en trouve plus
qui le soient davantage pour servir à leur preuve").[19] These
"primitive words" and clear principles are immediately under-
standable, although we are incapable of expressing them clearly
in words. But Pascal insists that these "primitive words" and
clear principles have nothing to do with the essence of things.
They just guarantee "the relationship between the thing and its
name in such a way that when confronted with the expression,
*time,* all of us direct our thought toward the same object. . . . definitions exist only to designate the things we name, not to show their
nature" ("le rapport entre le nom et la chose; en sorte qu'à cette
expression, *temps,* tous portent la pensée vers le même objet. . . . les
définitions ne sont faites que pour désigner les choses que l'on
nomme, et non pas pour en montrer la nature").[20] If the reference

points are not connected to an essence, they are probably not
linked to the third order. They do not give access to truth and
cannot provide a real escape.

Thus no natural support can free the hermeneutic circle from
spinning endlessly around its own axis. Reason, then, seems un-
avoidably bound by the hermeneutic circle. To clarify words rationally only obscures them. In the *Pensées*, Pascal also articulates
his distrust of rational language: "It is therefore odd that we cannot
define these things without obscuring them. We talk about them
all the time. We assume that everyone conceives of them in the
same way. But that is a gratuitous assumption, because we have
no proof that it is so" ("C'est donc une chose étrange qu'on ne
peut définir ces choses sans les obscurcir. Nous en parlons à toute
heure. Nous supposons que tous les conçoivent de même sorte.
Mais nous le supposons bien gratuitement, car nous n'en avons
aucune preuve" [S141, L109, B392]). Defining words embroils
us in labyrinthine verbal networks that strangle meaning. By
stumbling on its own successiveness and on the exigencies of time,
reason creates a sense of its mediacy and its distance from truth,
which are qualities of our sinfulness.

## "The Continual Reversal of Pro and Con"

Given that reason is successive, a quality linked to our sinful state,
Pascal emphasizes rather than disguises this shadowy underside
of reason. He accentuates the successiveness of reason by highlighting the rational problems of its relation to order. A specific
form of successiveness is the creation of multiple perspectives that
cannot be encompassed in one vision. Reason can grasp fragments
of knowledge only in a sequential pattern. The Pascalian narrator
explodes reason's aspirations to totality through "the continual
reversal of pro and con" ("le renversement continuel du pour au
contre"), a narrative structure that deliberately undermines the
readers' confidence in their ability to grasp a coherent whole.
"The constant reversal of pro and con" unveils a succession of
reversals between a given set of polarities implicit in reason:

> *The Reason of Effects.* The Continual Reversal of Pro and Con.
> We have thus shown that man is vain to pay so much attention
> to things that are not essential. And all these opinions are refuted.

Then we showed that all these opinions are perfectly sound and that, because all these examples of vanity are perfectly justified, ordinary people are not so vain as they are said to be. And thus we have refuted the opinion which refuted that of the people.

But we must now refute this last proposition and show that it is still true that the people are vain, although their opinions are sound, because they do not see where truth lies and always place it where it is not, with the result that their opinions are always thoroughly wrong and unsound.

*Raison des effets.* Renversement continuel du pour au contre.

Nous avons donc montré que l'homme est vain par l'estime qu'il fait des choses qui ne sont point essentielles. Et toutes ces opinions sont détruites.

Nous avons montré ensuite que toutes ces opinions sont très saines, et qu'ainsi toutes ces vanités étant très bien fondées, le peuple n'est pas si vain qu'on dit. Et ainsi nous avons détruit l'opinion qui détruisait celle du peuple.

Mais il faut détruire maintenant cette· dernière proposition et montrer qu'il demeure toujours vrai que le peuple est vain, quoique ses opinions soient saines, parce qu'il n'en sent pas la vérité où elle est et que la mettant où elle n'est pas, ses opinions sont toujours très fausses et très malsaines [S127, L93, B328].

The above fragment is constructed on the axis of the vanity or sanity of opinions. The narrator expresses a judgment from one perspective—that opinions of people are vain—but immediately changes his perspective, which entails a corresponding alteration in his initial judgment. The second judgment—that these opinions are not totally vain—cancels out the first one, but the second is then superseded by yet another one. The narrator gives the impression at the end of the fragment of having reached a final position: the people are indeed vain, although their opinions, in fact, are reasonable, because they lack consciousness of the truth of their opinions.

Yet this "final truth" is also questioned by the very fact that the narrator articulates his consciousness of the lack of consciousness. His vanity is not really different from that of the people: "Vanity is so firmly anchored in man's heart that a soldier, a cad, a cook, a thief, boast and want to have admirers, and even philosophers want them; those who write against it want to have

the glory of having written well, those who read them want to
have the glory of having read them, and perhaps I who write this
want the same thing, perhaps my readers . . . " ("La vanité est
si ancrée dans le coeur de l'homme qu'un soldat, un goujat, un
cuisinier, un crocheteur se vante et veut avoir ses admirateurs et
les philosophes mêmes en veulent, et ceux qui écrivent contre
veulent avoir la gloire d'avoir bien écrit, et ceux qui les lisent veulent avoir la gloire de les avoir lus, et moi qui écris ceci ai peut-être
cette envie, et peut-être que ceux qui le liront . . . " [S520, L627,
B150]). The narrator, conscious of his own vanity, is clearly inside
the circle of vanity: he is no more conscious of where the truth
of his "opinions" lies than are the people. Theoretically, then,
"the continual reversal of pro and con" continues infinitely. "At
the end of each truth, it is necessary to add that we remember
the opposite truth" ("A la fin de chaque vérité, il faut ajouter
qu'on se souvient de la vérité opposée" [S479, L576, B567]).

The narrator perpetually reverses the perspective, unsettling
those who expect to find rational and logical consistency in the
text. Every statement can be transformed into its opposite by twist-
ing the object around so that it revolves on a new axis. The shifts
in perspective play out the movement of a fall from truth into error.
The readers seek to locate a perspective of truth in order to arrange
the parts in a hierarchical structure that will provide an interpretive key. No sooner do the readers posit a hierarchical model,
however, than it rotates on its own axis, undoing the old one,
illuminating its error, and forming a new one. In this way, the
text thwarts the attempts of reason to grasp its essential meaning,
thus subverting the order of reason.

Although the Pascalian system may, in fact, constitute a totality,
it does not reveal itself to reason. Within rational discourse, there
can be no absolute truth to orient the readers' perspective: "When
we want to correct somebody usefully and show him he is wrong,
we must see from what point of view he is approaching the matter,
for it is usually right from that point of view; although we must
admit this, we must show him the point of view from which it is
wrong" ["Quand on veut reprendre avec utilité, et montrer à un
autre qu'il se trompe, il faut observer par quel côté il envisage la
chose, car elle est vraie ordinairement de ce côté-là, et lui avouer
cette vérité, mais lui découvrir le côté par où elle est fausse"

[S579, L701, B9]). The reading process that operates within the rational discourse of the second order plays out the movement of the fall. Reason can seize only a small segment of the whole, which the readers assume represents the true perspective. But the narrator introduces a new perspective to bring out a previously hidden aspect. Each shift reveals the insufficiency and error of the previous perspective. Because of the rapid succession of different perspectives, our rational faculties cannot comprehend more than one perspective at a time. The successive juxtaposition of perspectives, instead of adding up to a continuous chain leading out toward a transcendent truth, creates a discontinuity that undermines such a possibility. It becomes impossible to fix a hierarchy of values to discover a transcendent truth. All attempts of rational discourse to reason its way out of the hermeneutic circle only turn back on themselves to demonstrate the impossibility of discovering a transcendent truth.

The narrator criticizes reason because there can be no true proposition; each statement can be reversed to suggest its opposite which is equally true: "How ludicrous is reason, blown with a breath in every direction!" ("Plaisante raison qu'un vent manie et à tous sens!" [S78, L44, B82]). For Pascal, then, the true objective of reason is to underscore its own limits: "Reason's last step is to recognize that there are an infinite number of things that go beyond it. It is feeble only if it does not go so far as to realize this fact" ("La dernière démarche de la raison est de reconnaître qu'il y a une infinité de choses qui la surpassent. Elle n'est que faible, si elle ne va jusqu'à connaître cela" [S220, L188, B267]). "There is nothing so consistent with reason as this denial of reason" ("Il n'y a rien de si conforme à la raison que ce désaveu de la raison" [S213, L182, B272]). When reason reaches its limits, it can open up to what is communicated from the other orders.

## DISCOURSES OF THE FIRST ORDER OF THE BODY

Pascal's discourse on the body provides an explanation for the reversibility of reason's propositions. According to Pascal, the body is a discourse constituted by convention and arbitrary orderings of signifiers. The discourse of the body reduces all of reason's propositions to its conventional systems. Reason is trapped within conventional semiological codes and structures that one mistakenly identifies as the truth. By highlighting the fact that these codes are simply codes, the discourse of the body suggests that no perspective is inherently superior to any other. All rational statements can therefore be reversed. The discourse of the body thus not only puts in question the desire of the second order's discourse of the mind to arrive at a transcendent truth; it also helps reason to explain why this desire will always be frustrated.

Although the first order's discourse of the body highlights the fall of the second order's discourse of the mind into language, it is only reason's discourse on the body which can be conscious of this fall. Reason alone has the capacity to recognize that it is caught in the body's semiological codes and structures and is thus imprisoned in the hermeneutic circle. Reason can transcend its codes to be conscious of its entrapment in them and of its error. By revealing the conventional nature of codes that create the illusion of reason, the discourse of the body opens up reason to the fact that there may be more than one code. In this way, Pascal's discourse on the body opens up reason to rhetoric. It is the rhetorical nature of language, allowing for alternative codes, which leaves open the possibility of meanings outside our conventional human systems. Only at this point can humans look for something beyond human codes.

### The Discourse of the Machine

The first order's major discourse is that of the machine. The machine is a substitute for the apparent absence of a rational order. Readers bring to their search for God a precise set of mental dispositions, with a bias toward intellectual understanding for which clarity is the mark of truth. Reason, however, is not adequate for such a search in a world where God is silent and has removed evident signs of his existence. The narrator thus proposes an alternative approach:

> Order.
> A letter of exhortation to a friend to induce him to seek. He will reply: But what good will seeking do me? Nothing comes of it.

Answer: Do not despair. Then he would say that he would be happy to find some light. But according to this religion, it would do him no good even if he did believe in this way. And thus he would prefer not to look. The answer to that is: The Machine.

> Ordre. Une lettre d'exhortation à un ami pour le porter à chercher. Et il répondra: mais à quoi me servira de chercher, rien ne paraît. Et lui répondre: ne désesperez pas. Et il répondrait qu'il serait heureux de trouver quelque lumière. Mais que selon cette religion même quand il croirait ainsi cela ne lui servirait de rien. Et qu'ainsi il aime autant ne point chercher. Et à cela lui répondre: La Machine [S39, L5, B247].

"The Machine" is an alternative to the failure of the readers' reason which cannot find signposts orienting their search for God.

The narrator describes the human body as a machine[21] that is formed by custom:

> For we must make no mistake about ourselves; we are as much automaton as mind. As a result, demonstration is not the only instrument for convincing us. How few things can be demonstrated! Proofs convince only the mind; habit provides the strongest and most believable proofs. Habit inclines the automaton, which leads the mind unconsciously along with it. Who ever proved that it will be dawn tomorrow, and that we shall die? It is, then, habit that convinces us and makes so many Christians.

> Car il ne faut pas se méconnaître, nous sommes automate autant qu'esprit. Et de là vient que l'instrument par lequel la persuasion se fait n'est pas la seule démonstration. Combien y a-(t)il peu de choses démontrées! Les preuves ne convainquent que l'esprit, la coutume fait nos preuves les plus fortes et les plus crues. Elle incline l'automate qui entraîne l'esprit sans qu'il y pense. Qui a démontré qu'il sera demain jour et que nous mourrons, et qu'y a-(t)il de plus cru? C'est donc la coutume qui nous en persuade. C'est elle qui fait tant de chrétiens [S661, L821, B252].

Just as the mind is ruled by the body, so the body is governed by a mechanical structure caught up in the trap of custom.

The machine refers both to human beings who function as automatons and to the conventional structure of their discourse. "After the letter urging men to seek God, write the letter about removing obstacles, which is the discourse of the Machine, to prepare the Machine." ("Après la lettre qu'on doit chercher Dieu, faire la lettre d'ôter les obstacles qui est le discours de la Machine, de préparer la Machine" [S45, L11, B246]).[22] The machinelike nature of humans and of their signifying systems is the result of a fall: the soul has fallen into the body: "Our soul is thrown into the body where it finds number, time, dimensions; it *reasons* in terms of these things and *calls* them natural or necessary, and can believe nothing else" ("Notre âme est jetée dans le corps, où elle trouve nombre, temps, dimensions, elle *raisonne* là dessus et *appelle* cela nature, nécessité, et ne peut croire autre chose" [S680, L418, B233; emphasis added]). The violence of the verb "thrown" suggests the imprisonment of the soul and mind in the body which mechanically programs human thought to think in terms of semiological codes. What the body discovers is the product of custom or chance. Yet language calls the codes natural or necessary and thus human thought is henceforth constrained to operate within codified bounds. The body, then, establishes our discourse, that is, our customary ways of interpreting the world.

Custom establishes our modes of perception and interpretation and is thus constitutive not only of human action but also of human discourse. The interpretation of signs and the acquisition of knowledge, rather than emanating from a direct perception of the nature of things, spring from a purely conventional system of signs established by custom. Humans are condemned to be like machines, trapped within the body of language.

> The habit of seeing kings in the company of guards, drums, officers, and all the things that prompt automatic responses of respect and fear has the result that, when kings are sometimes alone and unaccompanied, their bare features are enough to strike respect and fear into their subjects, because we make no mental distinction between their persons and the retinue with which they are normally seen to be associated. And the world, which does not know that this association is the effect of habit, believes it to derive from some natural force, hence words such as these: "The character of divinity is imprinted on his countenance."

La coutume de voir les rois accompagnés de gardes, de tambours, d'officiers et de toutes les choses qui ploient la machine vers le respect et la terreur fait que leur visage, quand il est quelquefois seul et sans ces accompagnements imprime dans leurs sujets le respect et la terreur parce qu'on ne sépare point dans la pensée leurs personnes d'avec leur suites qu'on y voit d'ordinaire jointes. Et le monde qui ne sait pas que cet effet vient de cette coutume, croit qu'il vient d'une force naturelle. Et de là viennent ces mots: "le caractère de la Divinité est empreint sur son visage, etc. [S59, L25, B308].

Meaning and knowledge do not proceed from the nature of things; rather, they result from semiological codes created by the habit of seeing certain elements continually associated so that their association eventually comes to seem necessary and inevitable. This habit forms a bond more solid than that of reason. The repeated coupling of kings with guards, drums, and officers leaves an imprint on the human machine which stimulates it to respond in the same way even if the initial conditions are no longer operative or even present. In fact, this habit of association constitutes one definition of the machine: it operates in an automatic way; it interiorizes interpretive responses so that it repeats them mechanically, independently of an outside cause.

The repeated juxtaposition of signs carves out an exclusive interpretive code; nothing is thinkable or possible outside the rigid confines of any given habitual network: "Custom is our nature. Anyone who grows accustomed to faith believes it, and can no longer help fearing hell, and believes nothing else. . . . Who then can doubt that our soul, being accustomed to see number, space, movement, believes in this and nothing else?" ("La coutume est notre nature. Qui s'accoutume à la foi la croit, et ne peut plus ne pas craindre l'enfer, et ne croit autre chose. . . . Qui doute donc que notre âme étant accoutumée à voir nombre, espace, mouvement, croie cela et rien que cela?" [S680, L419, B89]).

Any customary experience—no matter how illusory—takes on the appearance of truth and locks us within its signifying system, for the major factor determining the impact of an experience is simply the constancy with which it happens to be presented to us:

If we dreamed the same thing every night, it would affect us as much as the objects we see every day. And if an artisan were sure of dreaming for twelve hours every night that he was a king, I believe he would be almost as happy as a king who would dream for twelve hours every night that he was an artisan. . . . But because dreams are all different, and there is variety even within each one, what we see in them affects us less than what we see when we are awake, because of the continuity, which is not so continuous that it does not also change.

Si nous rêvions toutes les nuits la même chose elle nous affecterait autant que les objets que nous voyons tous les jours. Et si un artisan était sûr de rêver toutes les nuits douze heures durant qu'(il) est roi, je crois qu'il serait presque aussi heureux qu'un roi qui rêverait toutes les nuits douze heures durant qu'il serait artisan. . . . Mais parce que les songes sont tous différents et que l'un même se diversifie, ce qu'on y voit affecte bien moins que ce qu'on voit en veillant, à cause de la continuité qui n'est pourtant pas si continue et égale qu'elle ne change aussi [S653, L803, B386].

Given that humankind's relation to reality is governed by custom, it is not surprising that people may be viewed as machines manipulated by the cultural codes that operate around and through them.

By showing that meaning is determined by custom, by mechanical, semiological codes, the narrator demystifies the illusions created by the second order of the mind. According to these illusions, we believe that our thoughts, opinions, decisions, desires, and judgments stem from ourselves, from our autonomous reason. We further want to believe that our language is a simple reflection of them. The narrator demystifies these illusions, however, by disclosing the machinelike structure of humans and their signifying systems. Rather than control their language, humans are like machines acted upon by language. "Heel of a shoe. How well made that is! What a skillful workman! What a brave soldier! There is the source of our inclinations and our choice of careers. How much that man drinks! How little that one drinks! That is what makes people temperate or drunken, soldiers, cowards, and so on" ("Talon de soulier. O que cela est bien tourné! Que voilà un habile ouvrier! Que ce soldat est hardi! Voilà la source de nos inclinations et du choix des conditions. Que celui-là boit bien, que celui-là boit peu: Voilà ce qui fait les gens sobres et ivrognes, soldats, poltrons, etc." [S69, L35, B117]). Human discourse possesses the power to create certain desires, beliefs, and to induce an individual to adopt a particular mode of action. In Pascal's view, then, discourse is a major mechanism of control which shapes human desire and belief, while creating the illusion that humans are motivated by an inner structure of authentic desire and belief.

Although the portrayal of humans as machines, partly determined by arbitrary and conventional codes, does injure human pride and strips people of their freedom and dignity, it may ultimately help them to seek God. The machine can be made to serve the goal of persuasion; it can reprogram people to seek God. In the *Pensées*, the narrator advises the readers to adopt the outside behavior of a given attitude, to act "as if" something were true. By adopting the external comportment of a given position, some of people's internal feelings will slowly move into accord with their actions. First comes outer action, then comes inner feeling:

> Learn from those who were once bound like you and who now wager all they have. These are people who know the road you wish to follow, who have been cured of the affliction of which you wish to be cured; follow the way in which they began. They behaved just as if they did believe, taking holy water, having masses said, and so on. Naturally that will make you believe and will stupify you.

> Apprenez de ceux qui ont été liés comme vous et qui parient maintenant tout leur bien. Ce sont gens qui savent ce chemin que vous voudriez suivre, et guéris d'un mal dont vous voulez guérir; suivez la manière par où ils ont commencé. C'est en faisant tout comme s'ils croyaient, en prenant de l'eau bénite, en faisant dire des messes, etc. Naturellement même cela vous fera croire et vous abêtira [S680, L418, B233].

Act as if you believe and you will come to believe. The phrase, . . . "will stupify you," which has produced a great deal of outrage among Pascalian readers, need not necessarily be interpreted as negatively as it has been in the past. It is only by accepting one's machine nature that this approach to faith can be effective. By blocking out thought and letting the mechanistic side of one's being take over, one's outward behavior will be able to assume the dominance necessary to bring one's feelings into accord with it. Appropriately enough, Philippe Sellier, in his edition of the *Pensées*, gives this unclassified section on the wager the title, "The Discourse of the Machine."

Mechanical action is a response to the problematic nature of desire and belief. Those people who really want to believe in God are often unable to because they cannot simply will their own beliefs. Even if they compile a long list of reasons and evidence for God's existence (and Pascal admits that the evidence is not conclusive), they cannot force themselves to think and believe what they do not think and believe.

Pascal's new approach to this problem in his own text begins by stupifying us, by pointing out that our opinions derive not from reason but from custom or habit. But precisely if this humiliating view is true and we are less rational than we think we are, then we may perhaps have some control over what we believe—by manipulating our habits. Although Pascal, like Hobbes, adopts a lower, mechanistic view of humankind, paradoxically this view increases humankind's power over itself. If humans are malleable machines inserted in a structure partly controlled by custom, and if they will accept this fact and study it, they can find new means of ruling themselves. Their machines can open them up to the correct operator, God. The *Pensées* seem to be the product of this new awareness. Analogous to genetic engineering, this mechanistic view tries to use the new understanding of how the human mind works so as to find ways of changing its belief structure and give humanity a new structure, a machine that functions according to God's commands.

### Textual Machinations and the Manipulation of Desire

In the *Pensées,* the narrator makes use of the discourse of the machine to play on human desires and beliefs. The machinations of the text itself act on the individual from the outside in the same way that habitual associations play on human beings. The discourse of the machine does not seek to enlighten, to appear clear and logical. It seeks, rather, to create desires in the readers which will leave them open to the truth of Christianity. Desire figures prominently in the narrator's strategy of persuasion:

*Order.* Men despise religion. They hate it and are afraid it may be true. The cure for this attitude is first to show that religion is not contrary to reason but worthy of reverence and respect. Next make it appealing, make good men wish it were true, and then show that it is.

*Ordre.* Les hommes ont mépris pour la religion. Ils en ont haine et peur qu'elle soit vraie. Pour guérir cela il faut commencer par montrer que la religion n'est point contraire à la raison. Vénérable, en donner respect. La rendre ensuite aimable, faire souhaiter aux bons qu'elle fût vraie et puis montrer qu'elle est vraie [S46, L12, B187].

Humans must want religion to be true before they can see that it is true because their desires, their predispositions, determine the way in which they perceive and interpret signs.

The discourse of the machine seeks, through various means, to create a desire in the reader to look for the truth of God. Yet this desire is dependent on certain more immediate desires: those for certainty, unity, and order, longings that ultimately require God for their fulfillment. Whether or not these are permanent human desires, it is clear that they were particularly acute in the seventeenth century, which, in general, sought to master and control nature through the possession of solid and certain knowledge.

The *Pensées* aggravate the desire for certainty, order, and unity by rejecting all the values established by seventeenth-century thinkers and by disclosing the prevalence of their opposites. Since the narrator's own goal is truth, he describes his means of achieving it in terms of disunity and disorder, an aesthetic of obscurity:

I will write down my thoughts here without order and perhaps in a confusion not without design. This is the true order and it will always show my aim by its very disorder. I would honor my subject too much if I treated it in an orderly fashion, for I wish to show that it is incapable of order.

J'écrirai ici mes pensées sans ordre et non pas peut-être dans une confusion sans dessein. C'est le véritable ordre et qui marquera toujours mon objet par le désordre même. Je ferais trop d'honneur à mon sujet si je le traitais avec ordre puisque je veux montrer qu'il en est incapable [S457, L532, B373].

The highlighting of disorder in the narrator's discourse has four effects. First, it emphasizes the chaotic nature of the subject matter. To impose order on an inherently disorderly subject matter would be false and misleading. Second, it shows that all discourse is by nature mechanical and conventional and thus there can be no order. Any order that one chooses can be reversed. Third, it serves a specific persuasive purpose: the discourse of disorder turns the reader against the proud rationalism of Descartes which deludes itself into thinking that it can possess a true order. Fourth, it creates the desire for a transcendent order.

Similarly, the *Pensées* practice an aesthetic of the uncertain, which fuels the desire for a certainty it denies in the temporal world. Following the conventions of reading, one seeks to locate one's "readerly place" in a text: the spot from which one can interpret the parts that are presented and situate them within an ordered whole. The readerly place is defined in relation to the position occupied by the narrator, who theoretically controls the whole. In the *Pensées*, however, the latter continually changes his position and/or code which then requires the readers to shift their perspective and code, provoking, in turn, a shift in the aspect of the content highlighted. The narrator demystifies the notion that his fragmented statements give access to the whole of the text.

The narrator chooses at any given moment an angle that runs counter to the previous perspective he set up or to the readers' conventional perspective. "If he exalts himself, I humble him. If he humbles himself, I exalt him. And I always contradict him, until he understands that he is an incomprehensible monster" ("S'il se vante je l'abaisse. S'il s'abaisse je le vante. Et le contredis toujours. Jusqu'à ce qu'il comprenne qu'il est un monstre incompréhensible" [S163, L130, B420]). The narrator continually disrupts the conventional habits of reading and interpreting texts, refusing to allow the readers to settle into an illusory "readerly place" or a falsely clear relation to the narrator.

Because our modes of perception, reading, and interpretation are based on habit, and not on truth, the narrator's disruption of conventional habits serves to draw attention to the way they function. By deviating from the codes established by custom, the narrator brings these codes into sharper focus and creates a counter, subversive habit of seeing. He reprograms his language to expose its semiological codes as mere mechanical processes for the production of "truth." He thus increases the readers' awareness that they lack a code adequate to explain Pascal's text, which cannot be represented by any conventional code. This lack strengthens the readers' desire for a genuine certainty grounded in truth, not simply a conventional code.

The narrator activates a machine within language, deviating from the custom that codifies the reading process as a continuous sequence. The code of continuity is designed to create the impression of truth. According to this code, the reading of a first sequence of elements should set up interpretive categories for the reading of the second sequence and the second should retrospectively illuminate the first. Despite appearances, the value of each sentence lies not simply in the communication of a thought content but also in its formal aspect: setting the ground for future sequences and fulfilling expectations raised by preceding ones. In the *Pensées*, however, this logical continuity is continually interrupted and shown to be an illusion, as in the following fragment:

> Man is but a reed, the most feeble thing in nature, but he is a thinking reed. The entire universe need not arm itself to crush him; a vapor, a drop of water, suffices to kill him. But even if the universe were to crush him, man would still be nobler than that which killed him, because he knows that he dies and he knows the advantage the universe has over him. The universe knows nothing of its advantage.
>
> All of our dignity consists, then, in thought.

> L'homme n'est qu'un roseau, le plus faible de la nature, mais c'est un roseau pensant. Il ne faut pas que l'univers entier s'arme pour l'écraser; une vapeur, une goutte d'eau suffit pour le tuer. Mais quand l'univers l'écraserait, l'homme serait encore plus noble que ce qui le tue, puisqu'il sait qu'il meurt et l'avantage que l'univers a sur lui. L'univers n'en sait rien.
>
> Toute notre dignité consiste donc en la pensée [S231–232, L200, B347].

This fragment thwarts the readers' desire for certainty and order.[23] To start at the beginning—"Man is but a reed"—the metaphor of the reed immediately demands interpretation, especially as it was not a common image at the time.[24] It requires an interpretive shift that depends on elements that are specific to a

reed. Help, however, is immediately forthcoming, for the narrator
adds "the most feeble thing in nature." The readers, in attempting
to grasp the thought content, would then conclude that humans
are weak. As soon as the readers feel comfortable about having
seized a definite meaning, however, the orientation shifts to indicate precisely the opposite, "but he is a thinking reed," thus suggesting a different view. By virtue of their thought, humans are
strong. The readers' desire to maintain a fixed view is again frustrated, for with no transition the thought takes another turn: "The
entire universe need not arm itself to crush him; a vapor, a drop
of water, suffices to kill him." Then suddenly the sliding back to
the weakness of humankind is once again countered: "But even
if the universe were to crush him, man would still be nobler than
that which killed him, because he knows that he dies and he
knows the advantage the universe has over him. The universe
knows nothing of its advantage." The fragment ends with the
idea that human beings are noble because their reason can know
their own weaknesses, a conclusion that neither subsumes all the
preceding thoughts nor stabilizes a meaning. The power and sig-
nificance of human reason are debased in many other fragments.

By refusing to conform to the code of continuity, the narrator
indirectly creates the desire for certainty. He stimulates this desire
on two levels. First, he encourages the desire simply by changing
perspectives so that the readers are never certain as to the narrator's final position. On a second level, however, the perpetual shifting of perspectives runs counter to the reading code that sets up
an illusion of truthfulness and creates a new code that brings out
the weakness and error of the readers' reasoning powers. As a
result, the readers' attention is drawn to the fact that the mechanisms guiding human thought are simply conventions. To the
extent that the readers are aware of them, they will be led to open
up to those mechanisms in language that lead them to seek a true
certainty outside their conventional codes.

## The Body of Language: The Signifier

The *Pensées* provoke the desire for a transcendent truth, not only
by continually shifting perspective but also by drawing attention
to the mechanical and corporeal nature of their language. To the
extent that language reveals the palpable and material character

that corrupts the perfection of its meaning, we are to experience it as sin (the body). Pascal quotes the immortal words of Saint Paul, "the letter kills" ("la lettre tue" [S299, L268, B683]). Once we become aware of the sinfulness of language, we will aspire to escape its carnality and to arrive at the purity of a transcendent truth that language cannot express. The narrator focuses on the body of language, the signifier, by departing from another important presupposition of classical semiological codes. According to these codes, the signifier should remove all traces of its existence so that the signified will seem to present itself in its purity, uncontaminated by the body of language. Deviating from this convention, the narrator plays with the signifier in a way that draws attention to its materiality. Frequently words are chosen not so much for their signified as for their signifier, for their material sense impression. The narrator makes striking use, for example, of the repetition of sounds. Repetition makes us conscious of the linguistic nature of our universe; all is fabricated through language. It corresponds to what Todorov calls the function of the new rhetoric, "to make us aware of the existence of discourse, . . . to describe the perceptible aspect of human discourse."[25] By highlighting the impact of discursive forms, repetition is language's way of reminding us of our captivity in the hermeneutic circle. It thus stimulates a desire to escape the circle and arrive at a transcendent truth.

Pascal's interest in the signifier focuses, for example, on the acoustic quality of language. Jean-Jacques Demorest notes that what governed many of Pascal's variants is not simply a concern for meaning but also for sound: "While working on his sentences, Pascal does not necessarily escape the fascination of their musical qualities. Meaning does not always control its form. In certain obvious instances, the autonomous power of words, their sounds, account for the variants."[26] Demorest further notes that Pascal composed many of his fragments aloud so as to pay special attention to their aural features.

Sounds are repeated through the use of assonance and homonyms, the repetition of different forms of the same words such as antanaclasis and derivation, and the repetition of the same word in a chiastic structure. Repetition also occurs implicitly in the figure of gradation wherein the same signified is repeated through the accumulation of similar signifiers.

On a basic level, the impact of the signifier lies in the insistence of assonance. Pascal uses paronomasia, a form of assonance, which involves the repetition of analogous sonorities within a given phrase. The same sounds are integrated into units with very different meanings.

> . . . the sight of *cats*, or *rats*, or the crunching of a *coal*, is enough to unhinge reason. [Note: the assonance is lost in translation.]

> . . . la vue des *chats*, des *rats*, l'écrasement d'un char*bon*, etc. emportent la rai*son* hors des *gonds* [S78, L44, B82; emphasis added].

> Diversity is as abundant as all the tones of voice, ways of walk*ing*, cough*ing*, blow*ing* one's nose, sneez*ing* . . .

> La diversité est si ample que tous les tons de voix, tous les march*ers*, touss*ers*, mouch*ers*, éternu*ers* . . . [S465, L558, B114; emphasis added].

> Lower your eyes toward the ground, puny worm that you are, and look at the beast whose companion you are. [Note: the assonance is lost in translation.]

> Baissez vos yeux *vers* la *terre*, chétif *ver* que vous *êtes*, et regardez les *bêtes* dont vous *êtes* le compagnon [S683, L430, B431; emphasis added].

Here the words seem to be chosen less for the cognitive function of the signified than for the affective aspect of their signifier. The paronomasia is extended by the play upon, not one sound, but two different ones.

Homonyms are also frequently used in the *Pensées*. In addition to the preceding fragment (*vers . . . ver*), consider " . . . *faute* des vrais objets il *faut* qu'ils s'attachent aux *faux*" (S544, L661, B81; emphasis added); and " . . . au *lieu* que les *lieux* où il est découvert sont univoques et ne peuvent convenir qu'au sens spirituel" (S738, L502, B571; emphasis added). (Note: I do not translate here because the homonyms are lost in translation.) That the Pascalian narrator was conscious of his repetitions is suggested by the fact that he felt the need to defend himself against potential criticism of their use:

When we find words repeated in a discourse and, in trying to correct them, discover that they are so appropriate that we would spoil the discourse, we must leave them alone, for that is the sure sign. And any attempt to correct them would be the work of envy, which is blind and does not see that here repetition is not a defect, for there is no general rule.

Quand dans un discours se trouvent des mots répétés et qu'essayant de les corriger on les trouve si propres qu'on gâterait le discours il les faut laisser, c'en est la marque. Et c'est là la part de l'envie qui est aveugle et qui ne sait pas que cette répétition n'est pas faute en cet endroit, car il n'y a point de règle générale [S452, L515, B48].

The *Pensées'* linguistic playfulness troubles the communication system and illuminates the material aspects of language. "By promoting the palpability of signs," as Roman Jakobson notes, "its [playfulness] deepens the fundamental dichotomy of signs and objects."[27] The palpability of language creates a new function for itself, one that is distinct from its traditional role of cognitive communication. Words are not simply neutral signs through which one unobtrusively passes to arrive at one's ultimate goal. Signifiers form their own patterns based on the interrelationships of their formal properties. They do not immediately open up to their meaning but resist being eclipsed by their signifieds. In a sense, a war takes place between the cognitive and the affective sides of the language, a war that favors the signifier and weakens the bond between signifier and signified. Signifiers can thus circulate among themselves, mechanically creating their own patterns and meanings without necessarily being grounded in a signified.

The repetition of sounds is one way of initiating a competition between the syntactical and semantic axes. If words echo back and forth along the surface of the syntactical plane, the place of meaning will be largely filled by this activity and the readers will feel less compelled to dip down into the semantic well of signifieds. Repetition diverts the readers' focus away from the semantic axis toward the syntactic plane by virtue of its monotonous and hypnotic rhythm; their attention is drawn to the quality of the language itself, thus delaying the perception of meaning.[28]

The narrator uses chiastic structures that also involve repetition. A chiasma is based on a formal reversal of repeated words on the syntactic level. A semantic reversal occurs in the following fragment: "Men are so necessarily crazy that it would be crazy by another twist of craziness not to be crazy" ("Les hommes sont si nécessairement fous que ce serait fou par un autre tour de folie de n'être pas fou" [S31, L412, B414]). This play of signifiers owes its force to the implied opposition between its signifieds, craziness and sanity, and to the shifts in the relationship between signifiers and signifieds. (Sanity is not explicitly presented but is clearly the pole against which the signified craziness is measured.) A reversal in the values attached to the signifieds and to their relationship with the signifiers underlies this fragment. All humans are so crazy that craziness, by dint of its prevalence, becomes a norm. Thus craziness is sane. Anything that deviates from the norm of craziness, that is, truly sane behavior, is crazy in this context. Thus sanity is craziness. What complicates the interpretation of this fragment is the fact that the word "crazy" belongs to two different semantic systems. It belongs to the old system where the opposition crazy/sane is operative and where sanity is the positive marker. We thus have statements like "it would be crazy," in which the word "crazy" maintains its old negative force of absurdity and ridiculousness. But the old system shades into a new one with the phrase, "by another twist of craziness." Although "it would be crazy" keeps its old negative force, it is now combined with another phrase "not to be crazy." Here is the pivotal point in the fragment, since the word "crazy" inserted in the new framework acquires a positive force. Craziness is the norm in this insane world. And the word "crazy," by simultaneously supporting two opposing meanings, demonstrates that very craziness in the act of asserting it.

The reading of the fragment sets up a paradigmatic frame of interpretation where the new, positive sense of the word "crazy" must also take into account the old, negative sense. In this fragment, the narrator is playing with the relationship between the signifier and the signified in such a way as to weaken their boundaries. He gives contradictory signifieds to the signifier "crazy" so that we cannot arrive at a final signified. The malleability of language only adds to the sense of its corruption. With its chameleon quality, it can bend to serve multiple purposes; it only emphasizes its lack of substance.

The signifier, as well as its relation to the signified, is further weakened in the following fragment: "Unable to make might obey right, men have made right obey might. Unable to fortify justice, men have justified force so that right and might live together" ("Ne pouvant faire qu'il soit force d'obéir à la justice on a fait qu'il soit juste d'obéir à la force. Ne pouvant fortifier la justice on a justifié la force, afin que le juste et le fort fussent ensemble" [S116, L81, B299]). As in the preceding fragments, the use of repetition is striking. The words repeat themselves in a chiastic structure: the two concepts of justice and force are first opposed and then their values are reversed. Again a paradigmatic frame is set up. Two opposing systems are superimposed on each other, an impossible ideal one and a viable but objectionable one: "Unable to make might obey right, men have made right obey might." The narrator takes up these two opposing elements and reverses their relationship. In the old ideal system, force should support what is just. In the new system, the relationship of force and justice is totally reversed, for force creates justice and does not imitate it. Force refuses to model itself on justice, but it takes itself as its own model and justice is then placed in a subsidiary position.

The perspective of the narrator is clear: force should be subordinated to justice. Force refuses, however, to derive its value from justice. It enters into competition with justice and becomes its own center, thus draining justice of support. In the end, the hierarchy is reversed and justice comes to accommodate force, finding elaborate schemes to legitimate the reign of force.

All the reversals in the discourse of the body, like those in the discourse of the mind, remind us of the conventional nature of our codes, as is demonstrated in the relationship between the signifier and the signifieds of "crazy" and "right." The narrator thus plays with the semiological codes that attribute a particular signifier to a signified, continually reversing our linguistic and rational structures so that we will perceive their codes as the arbitrary codes that they are and look beyond human signs. Moreover, the narrator's linguistic pyrotechnics, manipulating words to form repetitive structures and word games, delay the perception of meaning. Obstructing the immediate perception of meaning, language interposes itself, calling attention to the fact that we are all trapped in the codified body of language.

The notion that meaning is trapped in the signifier, the body of language, brings us back to the hermeneutic circle. Although it is language that encloses us within the circle, it is also language that provides a possible escape from it. Before we can transcend our fall into language and get back to the truth from which we have fallen, it is first necessary to recognize that we are indeed the captives of human discourse. Pascal's discourse on the body (whose arbitrary and conventional nature undermines all rational codes) shows that our lofty rational structures are imprisoned in the body of language (either formal semiological codes that mechanically determine thought, or mechanisms that break down those codes and make us aware that we are imprisoned in the hermeneutic circle). Although humans are beings of language who have fallen into the hermeneutic circle, it is only the discourse of the mind that can take cognizance of this fall. The mind's recognition of the *misère* of language's reduction to semiological codes also constitutes its *grandeur*. What allows the mind to signify the conventional nature of its codes and not be completely entrapped in them is the ability momentarily to escape individual codes so as to arrive at a consciousness that the human mind is not completely governed by its semiological codes; it contains an otherness that differs itself from all other codes. The discourse of the body thus opens the mind up to rhetoric, to the possibility that language can function figuratively. In other words, language is composed not only of semiological codes but also of figures that point back to the conventional nature of these codes. The very recognition of this otherness implies a level of transcendence to imagine the possibility of an Otherness outside language. One may wager that the intuition of this alternative comes from the natural light of the third order and that it can enable language to figure a possible truth beyond human codes. At this point, there is hope for Redemption.

# 3

# Two Stories of the Fall and Desire: Paradise/Paradigm Lost

## THE APORIA OF THE *PENSÉES*

Fallen from truth into language, we are trapped in the hermeneutic circle. The realization of our imprisonment in signs gives rise to two conflicting situations. On the one hand, it breeds the desire to escape and find a transcendent truth: "we burn with desire to find . . . an ultimate, solid foundation upon which to build a tower rising up to infinity" ("nous brûlons du désir de trouver . . . une dernière base constante pour y édifier une tour qui s'élève à [l]'infini" [S230, L199, B72]). On the other hand, it constantly reveals that we cannot attain a transcendent truth that would decide the meaning of our signs: " . . . at the end of each truth it is necessary to add that we bear in mind the opposite truth" (" . . . à la fin de chaque vérité il faut ajouter qu'on se souvient de la vérité opposée [S479, L576, B567]). The result is an aporia that presents two incompatible logics of our relation to a transcendent truth. The aporia undermines the belief that we can satisfy our desire for truth, as it becomes impossible to decide rationally which of the two logics is true.

The central dilemma in the *Pensées*, then, includes not only the fall from truth into language but also the desire to recapture the lost truth. The *Pensées* dramatize this dilemma in two incompatible stories,[1] one from the perspective of faith, the other from the perspective of uncertainty. The story of the fall from truth into language and of the desire to recapture truth is seen, from the first perspective, as an allegory of the historical Fall and of possible Redemption. Humankind fell from an ideal state of communication with God who guaranteed an unfallen, referential language. Before the Fall, signs corresponded to truth. Since the Fall, however, all language is constituted by figures that express something other than the truth they intend to convey.

The fall into figural language breeds the desire for truth. This very desire becomes, as I will show, a figure of both the Fall and Redemption. It figures the Fall by virtue of the fact that it cannot be satisfied, and thus it underlines *la misère* of our distance from truth and God. It also figures the possibility of Redemption because we are not satisfied with our fictions of truth; we desire to go beyond them in order to recuperate a transcendent truth. Our desire for Redemption suggests that we contain *la grandeur* of a former state wherein we had access to truth and God. The lost truth is the origin and goal of our desire. The story of the Fall and Redemption implies that its narrator has transcended language to acquire, through faith, the object of his desire: the certainty of a transcendent truth, of God.

This framework of faith, constituting one side of the aporia, cannot account for the whole of the Pascalian text, for it assumes a knowledge not available to humankind. Paradoxically, the historical Fall puts us in a state of uncertainty, so that we are unable to say whether a fall, in fact, even occurred. Trapped as we are in signs, we cannot escape the hermeneutic circle to gain knowledge of an origin from which we have fallen. Within the hermeneutic circle, all that humans can experience is a fall from the illusion of truth.

Narrating an epistemological fall from truth into language, the story of the Fall and Redemption literally throws the readers into an incompatible story, that of the fall from the illusion of truth. This story constitutes the other side of the aporia. Within the framework of uncertainty, the fall can never be more than a fall from the illusion that human codes correspond to truth. In their everyday world, humans can experience a fall only into the realization that their truths are but an endless series of conventional constructs. "What are our natural principles if not our habitual principles? In children, it is the principles received from the habits of their fathers, such as hunting animals. A change of custom will produce different natural principles, as may be seen from experience" ("Qu'est-ce que nos principes naturels sinon nos principes accoutumés. Et dans les enfants ceux qu'ils ont reçus de la coutume de leurs pères comme la chasse dans les animaux. Une différente coutume nous donnera d'autres principes naturels. Cela se voit par expérience" [S158, L125, B92]). On a daily basis, humans experience the dissolution of their belief that their codes capture truth. They cannot experience a fall from an originary truth, only from a paradigm of truth. "Whenever we think to have attached ourselves to any point that we believe supports us, it shakes loose and leaves us, and if we follow it, it escapes our grasp, slips past us, and flees in an eternal flight" ("[Q]uelque terme où nous pensions nous attacher et nous affermir, il branle, et nous quitte, et si nous le suivons il échappe à nos prises, nous glisse et fuit d'une fuite éternelle" [S230, L199, B72]).

As in faith's story of the Fall and the Redemption, desire plays a key role in uncertainty's story of a fall from the illusion of truth. Desire is, as I will show, structured like figural language that points in two opposing directions. On the one hand, desire supports the false semiological systems with which we represent the world. It allows us pridefully to delude ourselves that we possess what we cannot possess: truth and happiness. Blindly and mechanically, we pursue various activities that we are conditioned to believe will bring about the desired goal: "The reason why some go to war and some do not is the same desire in both, but interpreted in two different ways. . . . This is the motive behind every act of every man" ("Ce qui fait que les uns vont à la guerre et que les autres n'y vont pas est ce même désir qui est dans tous les deux, accompagné de différentes vues. . . . C'est le motif de toutes les actions de tous les hommes" [S181, L148, B425]). The desire for truth is also a desire for certainty, often the mere illusion of truth. Lost in the uncertainty of the infinite universe, we are led by our desire for stable structures to fabricate fictions of truth: "*we construct* ultimate [principles] which appear to be so to reason, and similarly, in material things, *we call* a point indivisible when our senses can perceive nothing beyond it, although by its nature it is infinitely divisible" ("*nous faisons* des derniers [principes] qui paraissent à la raison, comme on fait dans les choses matérielles où *nous appelons* un point indivisible, celui au delà duquel nos sens n'aperçoivent plus rien, quoique divisible infiniment et par sa nature" [S230, L199, B72; emphasis added]).

On the other hand, desire is never completely satisfied with semiological codes because it longs for a transcendent truth that its constructs necessarily falsify: " . . . it is necessary that the universal good, which all men desire, should not consist in any particular thing" (" . . . il est nécessaire que ce bien universel que tous les hommes désirent ne soit dans aucune des choses particulières" [S181, L148, B425]). Desire draws our attention to the conventional nature of our codes, which are cut off from truth. Although recognition of this conventionality in itself constitutes a truth, it is a highly unfulfilling truth. Consequently it points beyond the erroneous conventions toward a possible transcendent truth. In the perspective of uncertainty, however, the desire for transcendence can never be fulfilled because it can only replace one arbitrary code with another, which it blindly believes to satisfy its thirst for truth. What appears true is as illusory as a dream:

> No one can be sure, apart from faith, whether he is awake or asleep, given that during sleep we believe that we are awake as firmly as we do when we are awake. We think we are seeing space, shape, movement; we are aware of the passage of time; we measure it; and in fact we act as if we were awake. Therefore, as half of our life is spent in sleep, . . . we have no idea of the truth, because all our intuitions are simply illusions during that time. Who knows whether the other half of our lives, when we think we are awake, is not another sleep slightly different from the first?

> Personne n'a d'assurance, hors de la foi s'il veille ou s'il dort, vu que durant le sommeil on croit veiller aussi fermement que nous faisons. . . . On croit voir les espaces, les figures, les mouvements, on sent couler le temps, on le mesure, et enfin on agit de même qu'éveillé. De sorte que la moitié de la vie se passant en sommeil, . . . nous n'avons aucune idée du vrai, tous nos sentiments étant alors des illusions. Qui sait si cette autre moitié de la vie où nous pensons veiller n'est pas un autre sommeil un peu différent du premier [S164, L131, B434].

The desire for certainty leads to the establishment of codes we assume correspond to truth, whereas the desire for truth leads to the recognition that they are simply codes that arbitrarily represent truth. The alternate stories of faith and of uncertainty give opposing views of our ability to satisfy our desire for truth. In the former, this desire may be fulfilled; in the latter, it remains unfulfilled.

The mere existence of this aporia, which thwarts any desire for truth, seems to favor, by definition, the story of uncertainty. But even uncertainty is uncertain. If the readers could say that the story of uncertainty is, in fact, true, they would then have a certainty: the certainty of their uncertainty. The readers' desire for certainty paradoxically leads them to try to subsume faith's story of certainty under that of uncertainty as if the latter were true, even though it is based on a purely negative truth. But Pascal does not even let his readers maintain such a negative truth. Any certain statement of uncertainty will only fall back into the aporia and be subject to contradiction: "There is no rule, we say, that does not have an exception, nor is there any truth so general that in some instances it fails to apply. It is sufficient that truth be not absolutely universal in order to give us a pretext for applying the exceptions to the present subject, and for saying, this is not always true, so there are cases when it is not so" ("Il n'y a point, dit-on, de règle qui n'ait quelque exception ni de vérité si générale qui n'ait quelque face par où elle manque. Il suffit qu'elle ne soit pas absolument universelle pour nous donner sujet d'appliquer l'exception au sujet présent, et de dire, cela n'est pas toujours vrai, donc il y a des cas où cela n'est pas" [S477, L574, B263]). In this fragment, the speaker first states a rule of uncertainty: no truth can be certain, for there will always be an exception. His second statement, however, reflects back on his first one. It reveals that he has expressed the certainty of uncertainty. In order for the statement to be true and certain, there has to be an exception to the idea it expresses: all statements of truth are subject to uncertainty.[2] But if he could find an exception to the statement, then he could establish the possibility of an absolute certainty. For Pascal, all linguistic statements are paradoxical; they are neither completely certain nor uncertain, neither completely true nor false.[3]

In this chapter I examine the aporetic underpinnings of the

*Pensées* and show how they constantly throw the readers back and
forth between the story of the Fall and Redemption and the story
of a fall from the illusion of truth in order to bring out the vanity
of the readers' quest for truth in this world: "It is good to be tired
and wearied by the vain search for the true good, that we may
stretch out our arms to the Redeemer" ("Il est bon d'être lassé
et fatigué par l'inutile recherche du vrai bien, afin de tendre les
bras au Libérateur" [S524, L631, B422]). Depending upon which
side of the aporia we choose, one story appears to incorporate the
other. It seems impossible to read the *Pensées* without assuming
one story to be more true for Pascal than the other. Yet the text
is so constructed that the readers, once they feel they have discovered the certainty of a particular story, are thrust into the opposite.
They cannot help but realize that neither story is totally true and
thus neither can subsume the other.

   It may seem surprising to suggest that once his readers accept
the story of the Fall and Redemption, Pascal would seek to throw
them into the opposite story of a fall from illusion. After all, is
not the story of faith Pascal's ultimate goal? Although Pascal
wants his readers to believe in the Fall and Redemption, they
must do so in the correct way. To believe is not to speak from
the perspective of belief or to tell the story of belief. Like God,
belief exists outside narrative or any rational constructs. If the
readers were to accept the story of the Fall and Redemption from
within the bounds of reason, it would lose the mystery central to
religious belief: "If we submit everything to reason, our religion
will not have anything mysterious or supernatural" ("Si on soumet
tout à la raison notre religion n'aura rien de mystérieux et de sur-
naturel" [S204, L173, B273]). Pascal thus seeks to humble his
readers and to prevent them from falling into pride by showing
that access to knowledge of the Fall and Redemption cannot be
gained directly through human discourse and reason. Rather, it
must come indirectly through a growing awareness of the inability of our language to tell the truth. Pascal seeks to throw the readers outside the text by tossing them back and forth between these
opposing linguistic statements and opposing stories. True certainty can lie only outside statements or narrative, outside the
text with its rational aporia that keeps alternating between certainty and uncertainty, truth and falsity. The *Pensées* throw the
readers outside the text and into a nontextual realm of the heart

where there are no stories or statements, but where a certainty is at least possible. In chapter 4 I discuss the atextual origin of certainty.

## THE LOGIC OF DESIRE AS SOURCE
## OF THE *PENSÉES'* APORIA

The pivotal element accounting for the continual shifts back and forth between the two sides of the aporia in the *Pensées* is the figural structure of all desire. The desire for truth induces us to make statements about the nature of that truth, as, for example, "Thought constitutes man's greatness" ("Pensée fait la grandeur de l'homme" [S628, L759, B346]). This statement about human greatness, however, can capture, at most, only a part of the desired truth, according to Pascal, because it also points to an opposite, figurative meaning about human misery: "Everything that could be said by one side as proof of greatness has served only as an argument for the others to conclude his misery" ("Tout ce que les uns ont pu dire pour montrer la grandeur n'a servi que d'un argument aux autres pour conclure la misère" [S155, L122, B416]). In the same way the desire for truth and certainty leads many people to formulate objections to the proclaimed truth of Christianity: "Objections by atheists. But we have no light" ("Objection des athées. Mais nous n'avons nulle lumière" [S277, L244, B228]). This statement also points not only to its desired meaning but also to a meaning opposite to the one intended: "All the objections of both sides go only against themselves, not against religion" ("Toutes les objections des uns et des autres ne vont que contre eux-mêmes, et point contre la religion" [S690, L441, B201]). No statement can desire, that is, intend, a single meaning without communicating an opposite meaning. Since linguistic statements bring out a figurative meaning of their words—something other than what they expressly articulate—they will be able to state only a part of the desired truth. As a result, language makes us aware of a lack in its structure; the awareness breeds the desire to capture what has been excluded. The pursuit of this otherness, the truth that perpetually eludes human representation, makes us shift over to the opposite side of the aporia with the hope that it contains what is missing from the initial side of the aporia.

The logic that underlies the transformation of desired meanings into their opposites is that of *la grandeur et la misère* of humankind. Two seemingly polar states, human greatness and misery, continually point back and forth to each other through the structure of desire, which implies a sense of otherness. Because of our inability to satisfy our desires, we are in a state of misery, haunted by a feeling of absence or lack of fulfillment. The mere existence of a lack or of an unfulfilled desire is, however, not sufficient to make us aware of misery. Awareness requires a feeling: "One is not miserable without feelings. A ruined house is not miserable" ("On n'est pas misérable sans sentiment: une maison ruinée ne l'est pas" [S689, L437, B399]). This feeling and awareness of our unfulfilled desire, of our misery, do, however, point to our greatness: "It is thus being miserable to know oneself to be miserable, but it is also being great to know that one is miserable" ("C'est donc être misérable que de (se) connaître misérable, mais c'est être grand que de connaître qu'on est misérable" [S146, L114, B397]). Human greatness is constituted in part by the awareness of an otherness: the very desire for something 'other' that lies outside our present understanding implies that we are not totally enclosed within the codes we use to define our objects of desire. The otherness implied by desire creates misery because it makes us sense all that we are currently lacking. But it also points to our greatness because, unlike animals, we can be aware of our misery and imagine a better state. Within the framework of faith, this better state is a real and previous state:

> Who indeed would think himself unhappy not to be king except one who has been dispossessed? . . . People thought Perseus so unhappy at finding himself no longer king because the condition of kingship implied his always being king. . . . Who would think himself unhappy if he had only one mouth, and who would not think himself miserable if he had only one eye? It has probably never occurred to anyone to be distressed at not having three eyes, but those who have (no eyes) are inconsolable.

> Car qui se trouve malheureux de n'être pas roi, sinon un roi dépossédé. . . . on trouvait Persée si malheureux de n'être plus roi, parce que sa condition était de l'être toujours. . . . Qui se trouve malheureux de n'avoir qu'une bouche et qui ne se trouverait mal-

heureux de n'avoir qu'un oeil? On ne s'est peut-être jamais avisé de s'affliger de n'avoir pas trois yeux, mais on est inconsolable de (ne) point avoir (des yeux) [S149, L117, B409].

We do not have the unlikely desire to possess more than one mouth because we have never experienced the possession of more than one. If, however, we were reduced to being one-eyed creatures, we would then desire to have two eyes. Only dispossessed kings are unhappy when they are no longer kings because they sense a connection with a state that was formerly an integral part of their souls. Pascal concludes that if a better state exists, it must be a previous one we have lost but can remember. Otherwise, he asks, how could we know and desire it?

But what does the otherness of desire represent? Does desire imply the intuition of an actual past state wherein the object of desire was an essential part of our nature? Does it result from the loss of a former greatness in which we were, in fact, linked with God? Or does desire result simply from the loss of an imagined state of greatness? In this event desire would be the product, not of a former plenitude, but of lack alone. It would reside in human misery whose greatness lies only in its ability to project illusions of greatness and recognize them as illusions: "*Greatness.*—The reasons for the effects show the greatness of man in producing such an excellent order from his own concupiscence" ("*Grandeur.*—Les raisons des effets marquent la grandeur de l'homme, d'avoir tiré de la concupiscence un si bel ordre" [S138, L106, B403]). In the *Pensées*, desire alternates between representing the greatness of a possible lost state, a paradise, and on the other hand of reminding us of the misery of being cut off from such a state, finding only a paradigm of greatness. The story of faith dramatizes the former; the story of uncertainty dramatizes the latter.


## THE STORY OF THE FALL AND REDEMPTION:
## THE PERSPECTIVE OF FAITH

From the viewpoint of faith, the logic of "greatness and misery" does not constitute an aporia, for it is totally integrated within the framework of belief. It coincides with the story of the Fall and Redemption. The narrator assumes that we have, in fact, fallen from a former state of greatness, a prelapsarian state: "we recognize that [man's] nature is today like that of the animals, and that [man] is fallen from a better state which was formerly his own" ("nous reconnaissons que [la] nature [de l'homme] étant aujourd'hui pareille à celle des animaux, [l'homme] est déchu d'une meilleure nature, qui lui était propre autrefois" [S149, L117, B409]). "Formerly" is a time designated as before the Fall: "What else do this craving and this powerlessness proclaim except that, of the true happiness formerly existing in man, all that now remains is the empty print and trace? He tries in vain to fill the gap with everything around him, seeking in things that are not there the help he cannot find in those that are, though none can help, since the infinite abyss can be filled only with an infinite and immutable object, in other words, by God himself" ("Qu'est-ce donc que nous crie cette avidité et cette impuissance sinon qu'il y a eu autrefois dans l'homme un véritable bonheur, dont il ne lui reste maintenant que la marque et la trace toute vide et qu'il essaye inutilement de remplir de tout ce qui l'environne, recherchant des choses absentes le secours qu'il n'obtient pas des présentes, mais qui en sont toutes incapables parce que ce gouffre infini ne peut être rempli que par un objet infini et immuable, c'est-à-dire que par Dieu même" [S181, L148, B425]). In the prelapsarian state, humankind's first nature, man was "holy, innocent, perfect . . . filled with light and intelligence. . . . Man's eye beheld then God's majesty" ("saint, innocent, parfait . . . rempli de lumière et d'intelligence. . . . L'oeil de l'homme voyait alors la majesté de Dieu" [S182, L149, B430]). From this state of perfection and communication with God, humankind fell to the lesser state of "now," a time frame in which the readers situate themselves. This fallen perspective is that of humankind's second nature, where "man has become like the beasts, and he is so far removed from [God] that a faint light of his author hardly remains, to such an extent has all his knowledge been extinguished or disturbed" ("l'homme est devenu semblable aux bêtes, et dans un tel éloignement de [Dieu], qu'à peine lui reste(-t-)il une lumière confuse de son auteur, tant toutes ses connaissances ont été éteintes ou troublées" [S182, L149, B430]).

From this viewpoint the Fall may be seen as providing an explanatory framework for unfulfilled desire. The prelapsarian and postlapsarian states produce in humankind instincts appropriate to its respective unfallen and fallen natures. On the one hand, the instincts from the prelapsarian state create the desire to rejoin the unfallen state in order to experience unmediated truth and unity. These instincts are motivated by the memory of humankind's former perfection which hovers over the present state and prevents humans from forgetting the greatness of their previous state. Thus, despite the corruption of their present state, humans seek to "elevate themselves through the inner feeling that remains of their past greatness" ("s'élever dans le sentiment intérieur qui leur reste de leur grandeur passée" [S240, L208, B435]). "That is the state in which men are today. They retain some feeble instinct from the happiness of their first nature" ("Voilà l'état où les hommes sont aujourd'hui. Il leur reste quelque instinct impuissant du bonheur de leur première nature" [S182, L149, B430]). This instinct from their first nature makes humans desire something the postlapsarian state is unable to provide.

On the other hand, an opposing instinct from our postlapsarian state creates an incompatible desire consonant with our fallen nature: "they [humans] are plunged into the miseries of their blindness and their lust, which have become their second nature" ("ils sont plongés dans les misères de leur aveuglement et de leur concupiscence qui est devenue leur seconde nature" [S182, L149, B430]). But the memory of our former state of perfection haunts our current state of imperfection, thus reminding us of our corruption. Consequently, our fallen nature makes us want to avoid consciousness of our unfallen nature. Our amour propre, for example, goads us into constructing a social system based on the desire to obliterate the traces of our former nature which communicate our debasement: "we hate the truth and it is kept from us; we want to be flattered and we are flattered; we like being deceived and we are deceived. . . . [Man] therefore does not want to be told the truth. He avoids telling it to others" ("nous haïssons la vérité, on nous la cache; nous voulons être flattés, on nous flatte; nous aimons à être trompés, on nous trompe. . . . [L'homme] ne veut donc pas qu'on lui dise la vérité. Il évite de la dire aux autres" [S743, L978,

B100]). But the desire for deception and illusion is thwarted because an irrepressible instinct from our first nature reminds us that "human life is nothing but a perpetual illusion; there is nothing but mutual deception and flattery" ("la vie humaine n'est qu'une illusion perpétuelle; on ne fait que s'entre-tromper et s'entre-flatter" [S743, L978, B100]). Our current state thus embraces two warring desires, one emanating from the prelapsarian state and the other from the postlapsarian state, and neither of them will ever be satisfied. The conflict between the two desires is what Pascal calls "contrariétés" "two states of man's nature" (S273, L241, B765).

Despite the warring instincts of each state, there is no aporia when the conflict is viewed from the perspective of faith, for it can be explained by the shift from the prelapsarian to the postlapsarian state. Faith's story of the Fall and the Redemption furnishes a logic to relieve humankind of the tension of an aporia by offering a solution that accounts for both sides. It does so by explaining the relationship between desire and the Fall:

> We desire truth and find in ourselves nothing but uncertainty. We seek happiness and find only misery and death. We are incapable of not desiring truth and happiness and are incapable of either certainty or happiness. We have been left with this desire as much as a punishment as to make us feel from where we have fallen.

> Nous souhaitons la vérité et ne trouvons en nous qu'incertitude. Nous recherchons le bonheur et ne trouvons que misère et mort. Nous sommes incapables de ne pas souhaiter la vérité et le bonheur et sommes incapables ni de certitude ni de bonheur. Ce désir nous est laissé tant pour nous punir que pour nous faire sentir d'où nous sommes tombés [S20, L401, B437].

In the first three sentences of this fragment the narrator speaks from the viewpoint of uncertainty, according to which all desires must remain unfulfilled. In the last sentence, however, he shifts to the viewpoint of faith which provides a meaning for desire. Desire does not merely figure the Fall through the punishment of our inability to fulfill our desires; it also figures the possibility of Redemption and God, who created desire as a form of punishment for human sin and as a figure of another state of being from which we have fallen.

From the perspective of faith, punishment implies a punisher: God. God speaks to humans not through the signs of the order of his creation but through the message of his punishment which he inscribes in their souls. More specifically, the punishment assumes the form of a feeling, a desire, which communicates two different messages: the intuition of a former state from which we have fallen and the feeling of our present misery and inadequacy. Desire is presented not only as punishment but also as salvation: "we have an idea of happiness but we cannot attain it. We perceive an image of truth and possess nothing but falsehood. . . . so obvious is it that we formerly enjoyed a degree of perfection from which we have unhappily fallen" ("nous avons une idée du bonheur et ne pouvons y arriver. Nous sentons une image de la vérité et ne possédons que le mensonge. . . . tant il est manifeste que nous avons été dans un degré de perfection dont nous sommes malheureusement déchus" [S164, L131, B434]). Within the deficiency necessary for the existence of desire lies an image of plenitude which we can only feel, but which allows us to conceive of the possibility of salvation.

Unfulfilled desire, from the perspective of faith, plays a crucial role in designating and comprehending the truth of Original Sin. It constitutes "the mystery the farthest removed from our knowledge," which is the mark of "the transmission of sin" (S164, L131, B434). Yet "without this mystery [of sin], the most incomprehensible of all, we remain incomprehensible to ourselves" ("sans ce mystère [du péché], le plus incompréhensible de tous, nous sommes incompréhensibles à nous-mêmes" [S164, L131, B434]). Without the incomprehensible doctrine of Original Sin, the misery of unfulfilled human desire is also incomprehensible.

From the viewpoint of faith, the story of the Fall and Redemption thus seems to subsume and give meaning to the misery of humankind's inability to satisfy its desires, in particular its desire for a transcendent truth. Human failure to attain a transcendent truth because of the fall into language simply plays out the effects of the Fall from an origin, the prelapsarian state where humankind had access to the truth of God. Pascal thus establishes a cause-and-effect relationship between the story of the Fall and Redemption and the story of a fall from the illusion of truth. "Reason of the effects," an expression that heads numerous individual fragments, is the title of one of the twenty-eight *liasses* classified by Pascal. It suggests, in most instances, that faith's story provides a reason or an explanatory structure that frames and subsumes the story of uncertainty. Many fragments in the liasses state that the seemingly senseless misery of unfulfilled desire, as dramatized in the story of a fall from an illusion of truth, is not gratuitous; rather it is the effect of a cause that inserts it in a larger story whose structure gives it direction and purpose:

> From this principle which I disclose to you, you can recognize *the cause* of the contradictions that have astonished all men and have divided them into such different schools of thought. Now observe all the feelings of greatness and glory which the experience of so many miseries cannot stifle, and see if the *cause* of them must not be in another nature.

> De ce principe que je vous ouvre vous pouvez reconnaître *la cause* de tant de contrariétés qui ont étonné tous les hommes et qui les ont partagés en de si divers sentiments. Observez maintenant tous les mouvements de grandeur et de gloire que l'épreuve de tant de misères ne peut étouffer et voyez s'il ne faut pas que la *cause* en soit en une autre nature [S182, L149, B430; emphasis added].

Faith's story of a tripartite structure that links together a state of perfection before the Fall, the Fall itself, and Redemption provides both a cause and a transcendent solution, whereas the story of uncertainty allows its victim to spin endlessly in circles.

## THE APORIA OF DESIRE: THE SUBVERSION OF THE STORY OF THE FALL AND REDEMPTION

As part of the story of the Fall and Redemption, Pascal focuses on the effects of the Fall, in particular, on our imprisonment in signs and the hermeneutic circle that hides God. This effect, however, underlines the fact that the Fall and Redemption themselves constitute a mere story, an artificial, seemingly senseless construct, instead of a rationally founded truth: "Original Sin is folly in the eyes of men, but it is put forward as such. You should therefore not reproach me for the unreasonable nature of this doctrine, because I put it forward as being unreasonable. . . . For without it, what are we to say man is?" ("Le péché originel est folie devant les hommes, mais on le donne pour tel. Vous ne me devez donc pas reprocher le défaut de raison en cette doctrine, puisque je la donne pour être sans raison. . . . Car, sans cela, que dira-t-on qu'est l'homme?" [S574, L695, B445]). The story of the Fall and Redemption responds to the desire for certainty, for it provides an explanation for the uncertainty and incomprehensibility of the human condition: "Certainly nothing jolts us more rudely than this mystery, and yet . . . man is more inconceivable without this mystery than this mystery is inconceivable to man" ("Certainement rien ne nous heurte plus rudement que cette doctrine. Et cependant . . . l'homme est plus inconcevable sans ce mystère, que ce mystère n'est inconcevable à l'homme" [S164, L131, B434]). But if the story of the Fall and Redemption, like any story, is trapped in language, we cannot know whether the desire that constitutes part of its essence does, in fact, point to a former state of plenitude, a paradise outside language, from which we have fallen. The story of the Fall and Redemption, precisely because it is only a story, cannot satisfy our desire for truth, which can be only where language is not. The effects of the Fall thus cast doubt upon the truthfulness of its own story and throw us into an alternative one, which recounts our efforts to capture the otherness that the story of the Fall and Redemption necessarily excludes.

The alternate story of a fall from the illusion of truth possesses an alternate logic, wherein desire points not to the otherness of a former state of greatness outside language, but simply to a lack, an otherness within language itself, which holds out the illusion of a paradise that is always elsewhere. Just as verbal language contains a gap between meaning and signs, so, too, the desiring subject contains a gap between an object of desire and its representation. The true object of desire, which its signs can only represent, can never be made present: "Nature rendering us unhappy in all states, our desires project for us a happy state, because they link the state in which we are with the pleasures of that in which we are not. Even if we did attain these pleasures, that would not make us happy, because we would have new desires appropriate to the new state" ("La nature nous rendant toujours malheureux en tous états nos désirs nous figurent un état heureux parce qu'ils joignent à l'état où nous sommes les plaisirs de l'état où nous ne sommes pas et quand nous arriverions à ces plaisirs nous ne serions pas heureux pour cela parce que nous aurions d'autres désirs conformes à ce nouvel état" [S529, L639, B109]). Despite the desire for unity of presence, the desiring subject is always at a distance from its true object.

The desiring subject is conditioned by language to represent objects of desire according to inherited semiological codes. We imagine, for example, that the acquisition of money will bring the contentment we seek. But once we have the money it does not bring the happiness we anticipated: "Give him every morning the money, he might win that day, but on condition that he does not gamble, and you will make him unhappy" ("Donnez-lui tous les matins l'argent qu'il peut gagner chaque jour, à la charge qu'il ne joue point: vous le rendez malheureux" [S168, L136, B139]). The desiring subject thus becomes aware that his or her code misrepresented the true object of desire. The object of desire is not what or where we had thought it was. We thus represent to ourselves new objects of desire according to different codes: "we expect that our hope will not be deceived on this occasion as before. And thus while the present never satisfies us, experience dupes us and leads us from misfortune to misfortune until death comes as the ultimate and eternal climax" ("nous attendons que notre attente ne sera pas déçue en cette occasion comme en l'autre. [E]t ainsi le présent ne nous satisfaisant jamais, l'expérience nous pipe, et de malheur en malheur nous mène jusqu'à la mort qui en est un comble éternel" [S181, L148, B425]). Because all objects of desire are represented by conventional constructs unrelated to authentic expressions of a stable self, and because we desire something other than the objects that we represent, our desires can never be satisfied. The gap between the present desire and its possible future fulfillment remains constant. We project the moment of satisfied desire into the future: "the past and the present are our means; the future alone is our end." But because we desire what we lack, the future is a time "that we have no certainty of reaching" (S80, L47, B172). When we obtain the objects we think we desired, we no longer desire them because they do not correspond to what we imagined. The desiring subject never coincides with him or herself but is always thrown beyond the ever-changing conventional constructs and is nothing but a projection into a future that it never can catch up with. Life is thus condemned to perpetual futurity because what we truly desire cannot be contained in any object. Pascal's description of the perpetual deferral of goals to the future strongly resembles the Derridean notion of "La Différance."[4]

Our effort to satisfy our desires makes us realize that we cannot represent the true object of desire. Precisely because all desires are represented to us in codes, no desire can ever satisfy us because the codes will always misrepresent our true desire. Because of this misrepresentation, we must look to something beyond our codes. Although God is one possible object of desire, it is also possible that there is nothing beyond our codes but lack itself, and it is this lack that may be the ultimate object of our search: "We never seek things for themselves, but for the search" ("Nous ne cherchons jamais les choses, mais la recherche des choses" [S637, L773, B135]); "We prefer the chase to the quarry" ("on aime mieux la chasse que la prise" [S168, L136, B139]). If we desire only what lack makes us imagine, nothing can ever satisfy us.

The Pascalian "diversion" involves the paradoxical pursuit of that which we lack in order to avoid consciousness of our fundamental lack. Desirous of shielding ourselves from direct contact with the lack we experience, we seek diversionary activities and objects, "delights and games so that there should never be an empty moment" (S169, L137, B142). We crowd our existence with sports, games, wars, even literature: activities that block out consciousness of the gnawing sense of emptiness by creating material objects of desire: "When men are reproached for pursuing so eagerly something that could never satisfy them, if they replied as they should, if they considered the matter thoroughly, [if they admitted] that they sought in it only a violent and impetuous occupation to turn their minds off themselves, and that that is why they choose an attractive object to entice them in ardent pursuit, their opponents could find no answer. But . . . they do not know

that all they want is the hunt and not the quarry" ("[Q]uand on
leur reproche que ce qu'ils recherchent avec tant d'ardeur ne
saurait les satisfaire, s'ils répondaient comme ils devraient le faire,
s'ils y pensaient bien, qu'ils ne recherchent en cela qu'une occupation violente et impétueuse qui les détourne de penser à soi et
que c'est pour cela qu'ils se proposent un objet attirant qui les
charme et les attire avec ardeur ils laisseraient leurs adversaires
sans repartie. Mais . . . ils ne savent pas que ce n'est que la chasse
et non pas la prise qu'ils recherchent" [S168, L136, B139]). We
maintain the illusion that there is an object that could satisfy our
desire so that we can engage in various activities, diversionary
mechanisms to avoid self-reflection. At the same time, however,
we choose desires that cannot bring us happiness precisely to per-
petuate the sense of lack: "Only the contest appeals to us, not
the victory. We like to watch animals fighting, but not the victor
pouncing on the vanquished. What did we want to see if not the
final victory? . . . we like to see the clash of opinions in debate,
but do we want to contemplate the truth once found? Not at all"
("Rien ne nous plaît que le combat mais non pas la victoire. On
aime à voir les combats des animaux, non le vainqueur acharné
sur le vaincu. Que voulait-on voir sinon la fin de la victoire? . . . on
aime à voir dans les disputes le combat des opinions mais de con-
templer la vérité trouvée? point du tout" [S637, L773, B135]).

But the notion of the desire, of "diversion," as flight or pursuit
of lack is insufficient to account for all human desire. Humans
also desire the opposite: rest, which is elevated to the ontological
status of true being. Humans imagine that if they accomplish
their proposed goals "they will enjoy rest . . . they think they gen-
uinely want rest" (S168, L136, B139): " . . . the satisfaction they
lack will come to them if, by surmounting whatever difficulties
confront them, they can thereby open the door to rest" (" . . . la
satisfaction qu'ils n'ont point leur arrivera si en surmontant quelques difficultés qu'ils envisagent ils peuvent s'ouvrir par là la porte
au repos" [S168, L136, B139]). In pursuing rest through activity,
however, they seek, without knowing it, a false rest. True rest is
not attained through activity, which satisfies only their desire for
blindness. Nevertheless, their desire for blindness (through activity) indirectly expresses a hidden desire for the true rest that exists
only through an awareness of a lack that no activity can fill. With

this notion of rest, Pascal recalls its origin in the Bible. He quotes Ecclesiastes 24:11: "*In omnibus requieum quaesivi*. If our state were really happy, we should not need to take our minds off it in order to make ourselves happy" (S445, L889, B165). The relationship between rest and being developed by Saint Augustine has probably influenced Pascal's thought. In the *Confessions,* Augustine writes: "Thou hast created us for thyself, and our heart knows no rest until it may repose in thee . . . "; "With a hidden goad thou didst urge me, that I might be restless until such time as the sight of my mind might discern thee for certain." Rest represents for humans the ultimate desired state, the fulfillment of being, of what is mysteriously lacking in human nature and of which the present moment is destitute.[5]

But neither the code that represents to humans an ephemeral material object and makes them want to flee being, nor the code that prompts them to renounce material objects and makes them want to pursue being, is so successful that it can satisfy the totality of human desire. Thus, desire throws humans back and forth between the two. In the words of the narrator,

> They have a *secret instinct* that drives them to seek diversion and occupations outside themselves, which comes from the feeling of their continual misery. And they have *another secret instinct,* left over from the greatness of our first nature, which lets them know that the only true happiness lies in rest and not in excitement.

> Ils ont *un instinct secret* qui les porte à chercher le divertissement et l'occupation au dehors, qui vient du ressentiment de leurs misères continuelles. Et ils ont *un autre instinct secret* qui reste de la grandeur de notre première nature, qui leur fait connaître que le bonheur n'est en effet que dans le repos et non pas dans le tumulte. [S168, L136, B139; emphasis added].

At a primitive level, two conflicting secret instincts draw us in irreconcilable directions. They create an aporia of our desires. We alternate between the illusion that we can satisfy our desires and the realization that we cannot. The alternation between two opposing desires makes us realize that our representations of objects of desire are conditioned by semiological codes, misrepresenting that which we truly desire. The true object of desire is always elsewhere; we desire that which we lack. Because the individual is torn apart by competing desires, none of which can ever be satisfied, all human existence is condemned to the misery of unfulfilled desire.

Although one side of desire, a secret instinct which the narrator interprets as coming from the greatness of our first nature, is consonant with faith's story of the Fall and Redemption, the other side of desire, a second secret instinct which comes from the feeling of our continual misery, slips out of faith's interpretive framework and puts it into question by reintroducing the perspective of uncertainty. In the misery of our fallen state, we cannot be sure that the former secret instinct desiring a reunion with God and truth does, in fact, come from the loss of a prelapsarian state, that is, a desire for truth and not just illusion (diversion).

## THE STORY OF THE FALL FROM THE ILLUSION OF TRUTH: THE PERSPECTIVE OF UNCERTAINTY

Interpreted from the opposing perspective of uncertainty, devoid of faith, the instincts which supposedly connect us to a former nature may be a deceptive trick engineered by a force similar to Descartes' "evil genius":

> We cannot be sure that these principles are true (faith and revelation apart) except through some natural intuition. Yet that intuition affords no convincing proof that they are true, since having no certainty, beyond faith, as to whether man was created by a good God, an evil demon, or just by chance, and so it is a matter of doubt, depending on our origin, whether these innate principles are true, false, or uncertain.

> Que nous n'avons aucune certitude de la vérité de ces principes, hors la foi et la révélation, sinon en [ce] que nous les sentons naturellement en nous. Or ce sentiment naturel n'est pas une preuve convaincante de leur vérité, puisque n'y ayant point de certitude hors la foi, si l'homme est créé par un Dieu bon, par un démon méchant ou à l'aventure, il est en doute si ces principes nous sont donnés ou véritables, ou faux, ou incertains selon notre origine [S164, L131, B434].

Instead of being deceived by an "evil demon," humans may simply deceive themselves into believing that there is a truth, or a God. Desire may result not from a lost paradise, but from the loss of a paradigm, a historically prior illusion of truth which posited an ideal of harmony with the world. The *Pensées'* narrator is situated at a very specific moment in history which allows him to bring out the structure of desire. His century experienced the transition from one world view to another, based on the change from a finite world to an infinite universe. This moment is at the crossroads between what Michel Foucault calls the Renaissance and the classical *episteme*. According to the Renaissance *episteme*, nature spoke to humans through signs that situated them in a finite, ordered world, "linked together like a chain," which gave meaning to their lives. Foucault writes that "the face of the world is covered with blazons, with characters, with ciphers and obscure words. . . . [It] becomes like a vast open book; it bristles with written signs."[6] These signs point to God's will and establish a hierarchy of values. With the discovery of the infinite, however, comes the realization that the former paradigm was illusory. In the classical *episteme*, the signs of nature are believed to lead to error. Moreover, nature is no longer thought to speak to humankind because the infinite does not contain a fixed structure providing a grid within which its parts can find order and meaning.

### The Cosmological Fall: Paradigm Lost

The historical shift in paradigms[7] from a finite world to an infinite universe dramatizes the story of the fall from the illusion of truth and the creation of desire, discussed above. The narrator presents this story as a cosmological fall. He posits as an ideal the Renaissance paradigm based on a finite, unified, hierarchically ordered world which corresponded to the desire for certainty and truth. This paradigm also had behind it the weight of the Aristotelian cosmology, with which it shared many features. Aristotelian cosmology was also predicated on the notion of a finite world, all of whose parts have their place and meaning within the whole. The scientific revolution, however, revealed that the Renaissance paradigm was illusory by presenting a new one based on the infinite. The sense of loss results from the breakdown of the old paradigm. From this perspective, desire implies, not the greatness of a prelap-

sarian or previous state of truth and perfection, but merely the
illusion of such a state. Desire results from a simple lack, a sense
of loss.

The cosmological fall from the illusion of a true description of
the world dramatizes the impossibility of satisfying the desire for
truth and certainty:

> When I consider the brief span of my life absorbed into the eter-
> nity that comes before and after . . . the small space I occupy which
> I see swallowed up in the infinite immensity of which I know noth-
> ing and which knows nothing of me, I take fright and am amazed to
> see myself here rather than there: there is no reason for me to be
> here rather than there, now rather than then. Who put me there?
> By whose command and act were this time and place allotted to me?

> Quand je considère la petite durée de ma vie absorbée dans l'éter-
> nité précédante et suivante . . . le petit espace que je remplis et
> même que je vois abîmé dans l'infinie immensité des espaces que
> j'ignore et qui m'ignorent, je m'effraye et m'étonne de me voir ici
> plutôt que là, car il n'y a point de raison pourquoi ici plutôt que là,
> pourquoi à présent plutôt que lors. Qui m'y a mis? Par l'ordre et
> la conduite de qui ce lieu et ce temps a(-t-)il été destiné à moi?
> [S102, L68, B205].

> Why have limits been placed upon my knowledge, my height, my
> life, making it a hundred rather than a thousand years? What rea-
> son has nature had for giving me such, and for choosing this number
> rather than another in the infinity of those from which there is no
> more reason to choose one rather than another, as none is more
> attractive than another?

> Pourquoi ma connaissance est-elle bornée, ma taille, ma durée
> à 100 ans plutôt qu'à 1000? Quelle raison a eue la nature de me
> la donner telle et de choisir ce nombre plutôt qu'un autre dans
> l'infinité, desquels il n'y a pas plus de raison de choisir l'un que
> l'autre, rien ne tentant plus que l'autre? [S277, L194, B208].

The story in both fragments is a very simple one: the narrator
desires to understand the truth about his relation to the world.
This desire, however, meets with frustration and terror, not with
satisfaction.

The narrator's emotional response of fear indicates a sense of loss and a fall from a world view that told him he could satisfy his desire for order and truth. The sheer terror implicit in the question, "Why now rather than then?" and in the statements, "there is no reason why here rather than there" and "there is no more reason to choose one rather than another," presupposes a former world view, not a former world, which gave a precise reason for humankind's being placed "here" rather than "there." This situation refers not to a theoretical possibility but to the actual historical period when the world was viewed as a finite whole of which humans were a meaningful, integral part. The speaker thus evokes both the Aristotelian and Renaissance cosmos where everything was predicated on the representation of the world as a hierarchically ordered, finite whole. Of the Aristotelian cosmology, Ernst Cassirer writes: "It is a fact that all our affirmations concerning any concrete 'what' are always accompanied by affirmations concerning its 'where.' And it is also a fact that one cannot make qualitative determinations of physical bodies without basing them on local determinations. These facts must be interpreted by Aristotle in such a way as to confer upon place itself a definite and substantial meaning. The body is by no means indifferent to the place in which it is located and by which it is enclosed. . . . Every physical element seeks 'its' place, the place that belongs and corresponds to it, and it flees from any other opposed to it. Instead of a relative scale of size values, we have before us absolute values of being."[8] In describing the Renaissance cosmos, he says that "the integrity of the cosmos, this *concordia mundi,* would not be possible if a hierarchical *order* of the particular forces did not exist in addition to their mutual *interpenetration.* The activity of the universe not only maintains a definite form but shows throughout a definite *direction,* too. The path leads from above to below, from the intelligible to the sensible realm. From the heavenly spheres above, currents continuously flow down, and these sustain earthly being and always fructify it anew" (italics in original).[9]

In the above Pascalian fragments the Aristotelian and Renaissance world view is the lost paradigm of paradise; it represents an idyllic world where humankind's most fundamental desire for order and meaning was satisfied. All the givens of human existence—place, time, size, and so on—were not arbitrary; instead they were the products of a higher order, linking them together in a coherent scheme. The narrator in this fragment bemoans the loss of the paradigm that posits a spatial and temporal grid organizing reality in a coherent whole. The notion of a grid structure responds to two desires. First, it enables its parts to acquire value by assigning them spatial and temporal coordinates within its framework. The assumption here is that parts have no value in and of themselves but only insofar as they are integrated into a structure that transcends them. Second, the geometrical grid gives the world a recognizable shape, responding to the desire to translate the unknown world into known forms to make it "knowable." By bringing the world within human ken, the speaker is made to feel in contact with and at home in the world.

The narrator in the above fragments is terrified because he cannot satisfy his fundamental desire for truth and meaning, which is linked to the lost view of a finite world. The infinite, by virtue of its endless expanse, shatters the wholeness upon which his former world view was built. Faced with the infinite, the traditional ontological relation of the part to the whole becomes problematic since the parts are infinitely divisible and the whole is infinitely expandable. The part and the whole no longer stand in the same meaningful relation to each other; they cannot be naturally determined. They both become artificial constructs necessary to bring order to the chaotic, undifferentiated mass of homogeneous space. It thus becomes difficult to stabilize any constructed system to give meaning to its component parts. As a result, the desire for truth and meaning can never be satisfied, for it can never find a solid foundation. The narrator realizes that his former world view was a mere conventional construct demystified by the scientific revolution. He senses that all future orders will also be constructs. Gone is the illusion of a world that speaks to him and that provides a "home," establishing a hierarchy of being. As it turns out that desire was based on illusory codes with which we represented the world, all objects of desire predicated on such codes are also illusory.

Given the desire for truth, the narrator in the above fragments nevertheless does continue to seek the true code of his new universe. He focuses on two salient features of his world: (1) it is an infinite expanse of space; (2) it is a purely physical entity and as such it bears no relation to the narrator's inner world. The narrator is ignorant of the infinite immensity of space that surrounds him, and it, in turn, does not know him. Space is indifferent to human concerns. His selection of these particular facts about the world brings to mind the Cartesian metaphysical paradigm because it corresponds to an infinite universe from which humans are separated. In the dualistic Cartesian world view, *res cogitans* is cut off from *res extensa*. *Res extensa*—body, matter, external magnitude—affects the body in its mechanical determination, but it does not share in the inner concerns of humans. The world in all its infinitude does not establish a hierarchy of values.

The Cartesian paradigm thus demystifies the Aristotelian and Renaissance paradigm. Even though the conceptual perspective of the latter is rendered invalid by the infinite universe, its underlying theory of meaning serves as a backdrop, an idyllic world before the cosmological fall, against which the new Cartesian code is perceived. Because the old, idealized system established norms and expectations based on structures inherent in its framework, the new system will be unable to fulfill them. The narrator experiences the inability of the Cartesian paradigm to measure up to the expectations established by the previous model as a corruption of or a fall from a former perfection. Although the Cartesian paradigm may be considered more "true" on the basis of scientific criteria, the narrator is still emotionally tied to the illusory code of the preceding paradigms because it has an embedded history of conditioning his objects of desire.

The cosmological fall, like the historical Fall, is therefore created by the residual traces of a past whose lack conditions our desires in the present. The historical Fall, however, unlike the cosmological fall, is created by a lost world. Because this world suggests, in the perspective of faith, a stable, historically real state of being,[10] it is possible to recapture its essence and satisfy desires conditioned by it. But the cosmological fall is created by the loss of a world view, the realization of a gap between a formal representation of a past world and the present one. Since this world view is illusory, as are all human constructs, the objects of desire conditioned by such paradigms will also be illusory and thus incapable of bringing about true satisfaction. In the story of the fall from the illusion of truth, then, desire will always remain unfulfilled because it is based on culturally inherited codes, linked to former paradigms which misrepresent the true object of our desire: lack, or rather desire itself. These paradigms foster desires, needs, and expectations appropriate to their own framework, but which cannot be satisfied outside of them.

### Pascal's Demystification of the Cartesian Code and the "New Science"

As part of the story of the fall from the illusion of truth, the Cartesian code demystified the illusion of truth proposed by the Renaissance paradigm. It correspondingly set up a new code based on the certainty of science. It is this Cartesian world view that Pascal in turn seeks to demystify. From Pascal's perspective, Descartes and the believers in the "new science" sought to reverse the effects of the Fall and create a human-made paradise that would eliminate the notion of a lack and thus eliminate desire. They wanted to transform the paradigm they constructed into a paradise, thus eradicating desire through the satisfaction of all desire. For Descartes, humans, as "the masters and possessors of nature," can invent "an infinity of devices by which we might enjoy, without any effort, the fruits of the earth and all its commodities."[11] Because of the discoveries of the scientific revolution, humans no longer felt constrained by the limits imposed upon them by nature, limits that prevented them from satisfying their desires. For example, Galileo's invention of the telescope revealed mountains on the moon, new planets in the sky, new fixed stars in uncountable numbers, things no human eye had ever seen and no human mind had conceived before. All these discoveries gave Galileo the impression that he could transcend the limitations imposed by nature—or by God—on human senses and that he could learn how to obtain the objects of his desire. The new science provided humans with the tools that would allow them to measure, to weigh, to explain, and ultimately to manipulate the world around them. Bacon wanted "to extend more widely the limits of the power and greatness of man."[12] He sought the power to subdue the natural forces and turn them "to the occasions and uses of life" and to "relieve and benefit the condition of man."[13] Corneille's heroic ethic reveals the same concern with transcending the limits imposed by nature and achieving a state of mastery. In the famous words of

Auguste in *Cinna,* "I am the master of myself as of the universe; / This is what I am, this is what I want to be" (ll. 1695–1696). Control over oneself and the world required control of one's desire and will.[14]

The belief of the new science in the ability of humans to satisfy their desires threatened the Pascalian notion of Christianity. Although believers in the new science did profess some form of religious belief, their glorification of human power, reason, will, and autonomy nevertheless encouraged self-sufficiency and a turning away from the traditional view of God. The Pascalian narrator clearly perceived the threat posed by this self-sufficiency: "I cannot forgive Descartes: in all his philosophy he would have been quite willing to dispense with God but he had to give a fillip to set the world in motion. Beyond that he has no further need of God" ("Je ne puis pardonner à Descartes: il voudrait bien, dans toute la philosophie, se pouvoir passer de Dieu; mais il n'a pu s'empêcher de lui donner une chiquenaude pour mettre le monde en mouvement; après cela, il n'a plus que faire de Dieu" [L1001, B77]). According to Pascal, the God of Descartes and of many modern scientists is not a personal Being, the father of Abraham, Issac, and Jacob. Rather, God is a rational principle necessary to account for the creation. After serving this pragmatic function he can disappear, for all else may be explained and mastered through human reason. For Pascal the Cartesian notion of God is highly subversive because he exists essentially to satisfy the desire for scientific truth; he serves as a guarantor of objective truth. God exists, as Sylvie Romanowski notes, "to counterbalance error and to allow science to exist."[15]

As part of the story of the fall from the illusion of truth, Pascal demystifies the Cartesian pretensions to truth. He seeks to expose the delusions of grandeur of those of his contemporaries who believed that the new science empowers humans to transcend the limits imposed by nature or by God and to overcome their fallen condition in order to have access to truth. Pascal shows that the discoveries of the new science—which its followers claim as major tools in the pursuit of scientific truth—actually undermine its goal rather than support it. He thus uses the truths of the new science, in particular the discovery of the infinite, against itself to undo the notion of rational truth. Pascal thus develops the most extreme negative implications of the infinite. After so doing, however, he tries to recuperate them within religion.

For Pascal, the discovery of the infinite, the product of the new science, put in question the conventions that allowed humans to believe they could satisfy their desire for truth and certainty. The discovery of the infinite did not lead Pascal, or many others, to feelings of joy, as it did, for example, Giordano Bruno.[16] Rather, it produced feelings of terror. Even Descartes was not insensitive to its potentially frightening effects. His concern with certainty may be viewed as a reaction against the overwhelming fear of deception which he experienced as a result of the Copernican revolution and the discovery of the infinite; the new science suddenly revealed we had been living in illusion for centuries.[17] Many scientists were particularly resistant to the idea of the infinite because they foresaw the subversive consequences it might have for God's existence.[18] As Alexander Koyré argues,[19] Kepler's rejection of the infinite, for example, was based essentially on emotional fears of the threat it would pose to God's existence and the traditional relation of humankind to the world. Kepler, a devout Christian, saw in the world an expression of God symbolizing the Trinity and embodying in its structure a mathematical order and harmony. But it is very difficult to find order and harmony in an infinite universe. Kepler's fear of the infinite is expressed in his *De Stella nova in pede Serpentarii:* "This very cogitation carries with it I don't know what secret hidden horror: indeed one finds oneself wandering in this immensity, to which are denied limits and center and therefore all determinate places."[20]

Kepler's vision of a "secret hidden horror" seems to have anticipated the modern dilemma which Nietzsche carries to its logical conclusion: the death of the notion of God (the transcendent realm of value) means the death of the ultimate object of our desire. Strikingly, Nietzsche presents this death in function of the Copernican revolution and the discovery of the infinite. In *The Gay Science,* Nietzsche tells a story about a madman who runs into the marketplace, crying, "I seek God! I seek God!" When the people there laugh at him, the madman suddenly replies:

> Whither is God? I shall tell you. *We have killed him*—you and I. All of us are his murderers. But how have we done this? . . . What did we do when we unchained this earth from its sun? Whither is it

moving now? Whither are we moving now? Away from all suns? Are we not plunging continually? Backward, sideward, forward, in all directions? Is there any up or down left? Are we not drifting as through an infinite void? Do we not feel the breath of empty space? . . . God is dead. God remains dead. And we have killed him. How shall we, the murderers of all murderers, comfort ourselves? What was holiest and most powerful of all that the world has yet owned, has yet bled to death under our knives. . . . What sacred games shall we have to invent? Must we not ourselves become gods to seem worthy of it?[21]

By presenting the death of the notion of God in terms of the relation of the earth to the sun and the experience of drifting in an infinite void, Nietzsche suggests that the Copernican revolution and the discovery of the infinite may have played a significant role in killing God. In *The Will to Power,* Nietzsche writes: "Since Copernicus man is rolling from the center toward x."[22]

But long before Nietzsche, Pascal demystified the Cartesian illusion of truth by replacing it with yet another code: one that represents a terrifying uncertainty and anticipates the modern notion of God's absence. Feeling the "secret hidden horror" to which Kepler alludes and which Nietzsche's madman later describes, Pascal suggests that our most fundamental desires for certainty and truth may be incapable of satisfaction in a world cut off from a transcendent realm of being. The absence of God is indeed the drama of modernity and dominates the story of the fall from the illusion of truth. From this perspective of uncertainty, a hidden God is tantamount to an absent God, for he is silent and does not impinge on human concerns. God's separation from the world lies at the root of Pascal's question of language's ability to talk about and to know God.

Because of the uncertainty of an originary presence that could decide the truth of human signs, all discourse, even the story of the Fall and Redemption, falls back into an aporia between stories that both lead away from and toward certainty. The Fall and Redemption are interpretive categories that can be established only within the framework of human discourse. But according to this account of the Fall and Redemption, all human discursive categories are fallen into error. This implies that faith's story itself is subject to the same conventional codes of human discourse which are cut off from truth. Why should we presuppose that its paradigms of the Fall and Redemption are more true than those of the Renaissance and of the new science? How do we know that the story of the Fall and Redemption represents a lost paradise and not merely a lost paradigm? Pushed to its negative extreme, then, the story of the fall from the illusion of truth may be viewed as subsuming that of the Fall and Redemption.

Pascal, however, uses uncertainty's story of the fall from the illusion of truth to push us back into faith's story of the Fall and Redemption by weaving together elements from the new science and religion in a novel way. From the viewpoint of uncertainty, the new science undermines religious authority by putting God's existence in question. But from the viewpoint of faith, the new science supports religion, though not in the way its followers think it does. Pascal takes as a point of departure the premise of the new science: as a result of the infinite universe, a radical rift separates humankind from the world; in Cartesian terms, *res cogitans* from *res extensa*. The metaphysical situation of this duality lies at the root of modern thought.[23]

One of Pascal's major contributions to modern thought is his attempt to bridge the gap produced by this duality by resetting the new world of modern science within the compass of the Christian religion and its values. Although the duality between human understanding and the world has been used to question the existence of God or a transcendent realm,[24] he transforms this duality to make it support the notion of a *hidden* God. Pascal's God has withdrawn his presence from the scientific world as a punishment for the sins of humankind. Pascal thought the new science was entirely correct in bringing about the death of a particular notion of God: the Renaissance notion of a God fully present and accessible to humankind through signs embedded in nature. Nevertheless, the death of this notion does not mean that God is dead; it simply means that all codes (including that of the Renaissance) which provide a human-made logic for God's existence are dead. The new science demystified the code that allowed one to believe in God as an eternal presence that established a hierarchy of values for human life. Pascal believed, however, that one needs to discover a new kind of antilogic to allow for another notion of God—a hidden God. He believed that the codes of the new science, by questioning themselves, can become consonant with the notion of a hidden God. By disclosing the distance between humans and the world, with its signs of God, the modern world of the infinite can humble humans, thus reminding them of their fallen status. "If there were no obscurity, man would not feel his corruption" (S690, L446, B586). Obscurity lies at the heart of Pascal's notion of Christianity and God: "Recognize the truth of religion in its very obscurity" (S690, L439, B565). From this perspective the new science supports Christianity, for its reason undermines the Renaissance notion of God which held that he manifested his will clearly in the signs of nature. Pascal thus counters the threat of the new science to destroy God and reincorporates the cosmological fall and the story of the fall from the illusion of truth into the story of the Fall and Redemption.

## THE APORIA OF THE PASCALIAN "I"

Caught between two conflicting stories, the readers of the *Pensées* thus look to the author behind the "I" to help discover Pascal's true desire. But as the author's desire to tell the true story is not different from all human desire, which is incapable of accomplishing its goal, his attempt to tell the true story must fail and fall into a rational aporia. A major problem in determining Pascal's true desire, his "thoughts at the back of his mind" (S650, L797, B310), is that all we have are signs, words spoken by an unidentified narrator speaking from various unidentified locations.[25]

The history of the responses to this problem illustrates the aporia of the Pascalian "I." Many readers identify Pascal with those fragments that express doubt and fear. Valéry analyzes the art of the famous fragment, "The eternal silence of these infinite spaces terrifies me" (S233, L201, B206), and assumes that the "I" is Pascal himself, expressing fear and uncertainty.[26] Likewise, in Gide's *La Porte étroite*, the character Alissa, who is reading the *Pensées*, questions Pascal's faith: "I often wonder if his pathetic tone is not the result of doubt rather than of faith. Perfect faith has neither so many tears nor a wavering voice."[27] She does not find the Pascalian account of the Fall and Redemption convincing. According to Henri Lefebvre, Pascal is split in two and plays out two

roles, that of the nonbeliever as well as that of the believer: "Pascal
. . . engages in an extensive dialogue with himself . . . a dialogue
that is, at the same time, an interior monologue."[28] Albert Béguin
specifically takes issue with the tradition that identifies Pascal
with a particular "I" of the *Pensées*. According to Béguin, Pascal is
complete master of his text; he assumes many different voices solely
as a pedagogical and persuasive tactic. Béguin poses the problem:
"The true 'Pascalian' anguish is that of thought which is no longer
certain of dominating its object. . . . Can we still assign to man
a place where he can live without being overwhelmed, in a world
that is no longer to his scale? Pascal asked himself this question
with such insistence that one might be led to believe that he had
never escaped from his fascinating, obsessive fear." Nevertheless,
Béguin concludes that Pascal, at the time he wrote the *Pensées,* was
"already beyond anxiety."[29] Along with Béguin, the traditional
Pascalian readers identify Pascal with those fragments that express
faith and certainty. They assume that whenever a speaker expresses anguish or uncertainty, it is the libertine or the nonbeliever
who is speaking. And, correspondingly, whenever a speaker expresses joy and certainty in the belief of God, it is Pascal who is
speaking. This approach, however, unwittingly hides the fact that
the speaker is caught in the hermeneutic circle. It presupposes
that the speakers have a transcendent existence outside the text
which determines the meaning of their discourse. And yet it is
the very existence of such a transcendent speaker which the text
puts in question. Although the subject seems to determine the
meaning of his or her statements, the reverse is, in fact, true: the
subject is defined by textual statements. And because the textual
statements alternate between two opposing meanings, they may
also refer to two different subjects. For example, the fragment,
"The eternal silence of these infinite spaces terrifies me" (S233,
L201, B206), may express the terror of a subject who speaks from
the perspective of uncertainty. He is frightened because he can
find no clear signs of God's existence. Or, the terror expressed may
be only a terror tactic on the part of a speaker speaking from the
perspective of faith. The speaker may adopt the perspective of
uncertainty as a strategy to humble the readers and to make them
desire and wager for faith in God. It is the readers' personal interpretations of the statements which determine their choice of sub-

ject. In the *Pensées*, one cannot state with certainty who is speaking
at any given moment, for there are no assigned characters. One
cannot know with certainty what constitutes Pascal's true desire.
Because Pascal cannot prove rationally the truth or falsity of
either story, the wager becomes central to his argument. Desire,
not reason, is a key element in encouraging the readers to make
a leap of faith and believe in God despite the uncertainty of the evidence. After stating that man has "no truth that is either abiding
or satisfactory," the narrator continues: "I should therefore like
to arouse in man the desire to find truth, to be ready and free
from passions, to follow it wherever he may find it, realizing how
much his knowledge is clouded by passions" ("Je voudrais donc
porter l'homme à désirer d'en trouver, à être prêt et dégagé des
passions, pour la suivre où il la trouvera, sachant combien sa connaissance s'est obscurcie par les passions" [S151, L119, B423]).
Desire assumes paramount importance because reason, caught
in the hermeneutic circle, can never give any definitive evidence
of God: "The prophecies, even the miracles and proofs of our religion, are not of such a kind that they can be said to be absolutely
convincing. . . . As evidence must exceed, or at least equal, the evidence to the contrary, it cannot be reason that decides us against
following it" ("Les prophéties, les miracles mêmes et les preuves
de notre religion ne sont pas de telle nature qu'on puisse dire
qu'ils sont absolument convaincants. . . . l'évidence est telle
qu'elle surpasse ou égale pour le moins l'évidence du contraire,
de sorte que ce n'est pas la raison qui puisse déterminer à ne la
pas suivre" [S423, L835, B564]). The impotence of reason to generate belief does not, however, mean that it is unreasonable to follow dogma and act as if one believed. The desire for an absolute
truth can lead the readers to wager for God. It is not until after
they have made the leap, however, that readers will find an emotional certainty of evidence necessary to prove the truth of the
Christian faith. Once one is within the system, everything will con-
firm its truth: "For my part, I confess that as soon as the Christian
religion reveals the principle that men are by nature corrupt and
have fallen away from God, one's eyes are opened and the mark
of this truth is everywhere apparent; for nature is such that it
points at every turn to a God who has been lost, both within man
and without, and to a corrupt nature" ("Pour moi, j'avoue qu'aus-

sitôt que la religion chrétienne découvre ce principe, que la nature des hommes est corrompue et déchue de Dieu, cela ouvre les yeux à voir partout le caractère de cette vérité; car la nature est telle, qu'elle marque partout un Dieu perdu, et dans l'homme, et hors de l'homme, et une nature corrompue" [S708, L471, B441]); "There is nothing on earth which does not show man's misery or God's mercy, man's powerlessness without God or man's power with God" ("Il n'y a rien sur la terre qui ne montre ou la misère de l'homme ou la miséricorde de Dieu, ou l'impuissance de l'homme sans Dieu ou la puissance de l'homme avec Dieu" [S705, L468, B562]). Unfortunately, access to this realm of certainty and coherence is not possible through human codes of reason and thus through the *Pensées;* Pascal can never know whether he is generating a desire for God or a totally incompatible desire.

Buffeting the readers back and forth between alternate stories, the text seeks to toss them outside the text, outside the rational network of signs in which they are imprisoned, in order to look more closely elsewhere. The certainty they seek can lie only in the atextuality of the heart.

# 4

# Reading in/of the *Pensées*

Stendhal: "When I read Pascal, I feel that
I reread myself."
Proust: "In truth, each reader is, when he
reads, the reader of himself."
Lautréamont: "Plagiarism is necessary."

The *Pensées* throw the readers out of the security of a text with a
God-like narrator, just as they were thrown out of a paradise/para-
digm of truth. They fall into the uncertainty of reading. Just as
the readers of God's texts—Scripture and nature—are separated
from divine truth, so the readers of the *Pensées* are cut off from Pascal's true intention. How, then, is one to read the infinitely open
texts of a *Deus absconditus* which appear to be silent, not pointing
to any clear meaning or to their maker? And how is one to read the
*Pensées*, an infinitely open, unfinished work, the product of a *homo
absconditus*? Like the problems of knowing God's truth which result
from the historical Fall, the problems of reading Pascal's text
come from his notion of our epistemological fall from truth into
language and not simply from the unique circumstances of its composition, as is commonly thought. As we are trapped in fallen language, we have only signs of how Pascal intended us to read.
There exists no guarantee of an exact correspondence between our
interpretation of these signs and the author's intention. No reading
can be certain it has captured an authorial intention.

The fallen creatures who populate the world of the *Pensées* are all
readers in search of signs that point to God's existence, or at least
to a fixed structure that will satisfy their need for order. The *Pensées*
narrate the story of their attempt to find and decipher a system of

signs in the world wherein they can read God's truth. These readers hope that once they locate the signs and follow them to their
logical end, they will ultimately arrive at a pure, unmediated
understanding of God, the Author. But, in fact, their readings fail
to capture the divine truth. First, readers cannot be certain that
their perception of a sign system is anchored in the empirical evidence of the world and does not come from a projection of their
own conventions of reading. Second, their interpretation of this
sign system, regardless of its origin, falls prey to an uncontrollable,
rhetorical structure. It engenders an aporia that suggests meanings that cannot be resolved by any single semiological code. What
one uses to decide the proper interpretation of signs are more signs.
The effort to lift the veil of signs thus leads only to their prolifera-
tion, so that we can never be sure whether we are face-to-face with
the bare truth or with our (mis)representations of truth. If and
when genuine communication does occur, we may have no definite
means of recognizing it. All authors are hidden amid a morass of
signs, which cast their readers adrift. The awareness of this problem, however, leads to a new model of reading the divine, hidden
author's text, as well as for the *Pensées* themselves.

My goal in this chapter is to explore the implicit stories of reading dramatized in the *Pensées* and to examine Pascal's theory of
reading, which is the culmination of his theory of signs, figures,
fallen language, and desire. The crucial question is how readers
can read the *Pensées* and the world so that they will open up to
God. As I show, Pascal's theory of reading figures a fall of all
texts into signs and fragments that are cut off from the author.
But it may also figure a redemption through the unity of God's hidden authorship. For Pascal, all authors except God are deprived
of their sovereignty; they write in a system that writes them and
their texts. This authorial absence makes the readers aware of
their fall from truth and may ultimately open them up to God,
the hidden Author who writes all texts.

## THE PASCALIAN CHALLENGE TO THE
## RATIONALIST MODEL OF READING

The rationalist model of reading, rooted in Aristotelian theory,
establishes a hierarchical relationship between author and reader.

The author, acting as original source, inserts a unified and stable meaning into a clearly delimited text which it is the readers' task to extract. And though this meaning is embedded in the text, it may be removed from its envelope without altering its essence because it inheres in a fixed, objective grammatical structure. Although readings of the same text may be different, the rationalist model views them as progressive stages, each one unpacking yet another part of a unifying whole. From this perspective, authors are viewed as insiders, privy to a mysterious inner truth. The process of reading presupposes that the readers can decipher the text's codes that grant access to the inner circle, where they will share in the author's privileged knowledge.

The key image of this model is one of control, a control based on the assumption of a purely semiological language that can successfully subordinate the rhetorical aspect of language and guarantee the author's communication of only one unifying meaning to the reader. The model's second major assumption concerns the author as a conscious, full, stable being. In this view, the individual consciousness is a fundamental means of intelligibility and unity. It is the original, explanatory cause of the text it produces and has full authority over its meaning. Finally, the model assumes that the readers, as autonomous individuals, can wipe the slate of their minds clean so that the author can write his or her message directly on it.

Rationalists, who subscribe to the assumptions underlying this model of reading, argue that belief in God is contingent upon the ability to find objective signs that communicate his truth directly.[1] They expect to find an Author behind the world who seeks to speak directly with them. The readers' expectations, however, are inevitably thwarted because all they find is silence. They become confused and frightened when no such Author clearly manifests himself.

> I look everywhere and all I see is obscurity. Nature has nothing to offer me that does not give rise to doubt and anxiety. If I saw no sign of a Divinity there I should decide on a negative solution; if I saw signs of a Creator everywhere I should peacefully settle down in faith.

> Je regarde de toutes parts, et je ne vois partout qu'obscurité. La nature ne m'offre rien qui ne soit matière de doute et d'inquiétude.

Si je n'y voyais rien qui marquât une Divinité, je me déterminerais
à la négative; si je voyais partout les marques d'un Créateur, je
reposerais en paix dans la foi [S682, L429, B229].

Behind the famous piercing cry, "The eternal silence of these
infinite spaces terrifies me" (S233, L201, B206), lies a fallen crea-
ture who seeks to read the world by finding and deciphering signs
that will allow him or her to unlock the secret of the divine
Author's true meaning. But the world resists the establishment
of any semiological codes that would reveal a hidden logic; it does
not allow the readers to decode any clear message. They are unable
to discern any definite proof concerning either God's presence or
absence. If God does exist, he does not manifest himself through
human representations of his creation; he appears to be separated
from the world he authored.

According to Pascal, it is precisely the rationalists' assumptions
about reading that cause their disbelief and create their sense of
terror. Pascal suggests that they are not reading in the proper
way. First, they are looking only to the outer world which does
not contain the clear signs of God they are seeking: they are "people deprived of faith and grace, who examine with their light everything they see in nature which might lead them to this knowledge,
and they find only obscurity and darkness" (" . . . ces personnes
destitutées de foi et de grâce, qui recherchant de toute leur lumière
tout ce qu'ils voient dans la nature qui les peut mener à cette connaissance ne trouvent qu'obscurité et ténèbres" [S644, L781,
B242]). "But, you say, if he had wanted me to worship him, he
would have left me some visible signs of his will. So he did, but
you neglect them. Look for them; it is worth the effort" ("Mais—
dites-vous, s'il avait voulu que je l'adorasse il m'aurait laissé des
signes de sa volonté. Aussi a(-t-)il fait, mais vous les négligez.
Cherchez-les donc; cela le vaut bien" [S190, L158, B236]). Second,
they are asking the wrong questions:

Why, do you not say yourself that the sky and the birds prove
God? No. Does your religion not say so? No. For though it is true
for those souls upon whom God has projected his light, it is untrue
for the majority.

> Eh quoi ne dites vous pas vous-même que le ciel et les oiseaux prouvent Dieu? non. Et votre religion ne le dit-elle pas? non. Car encore que cela est vrai en un sens pour quelques âmes à qui Dieu donna cette lumière, néanmoins cela est faux à l'égard de la plupart [S38, L3, B244].

The narrator argues that although God does speak to us, he does not speak the language of reason which would be revealed through any system of signs. Consequently, divine language is not directly accessible to God's readers. To the extent that the readers find any order in the world, it depends less on what one may think to be "objectively" inscribed in it and more on what they project onto it out of the inner light given by God.

Pascal thus challenges the rationalist notion of direct communication between author and reader. As a result of our fall into language, the traditional authoritative structures, such as a stable, objective text and an author who controls the transmission of meaning, disintegrate. Pascal seeks to redefine the notion of text and its relation to authors and readers. What constitutes the proper text? What kinds of questions should one ask of it? In other words, how should one read in a fallen world?

### Saint Augustine on Reading

Pascal's own model of reading seems to have been inspired by Saint Augustine. Like the rationalists, but unlike Pascal, Augustine believed that the world is a preexisting text composed of signs that communicate God's message. This message is in the world regardless of who reads it: " . . . heaven and earth and all that they contain proclaim that I should love you, and their message never ceases to sound in the ears of all mankind, so that there is no excuse for any not to love you" (*Confessions* X.6). But, unlike the rationalists and like Pascal, Augustine believed that the message cannot be obtained by any simple "objective" reading. Rather, to obtain it one must have a complex relationship with a truth inscribed in one's soul. Augustine continues: "Surely everyone whose senses are not impaired is aware of the universe around him? Why, then, does it not give the same message to us all? . . . It would be nearer the truth to say that it gives an answer to all,

but it is only understood by those who compare the message it
gives them through their senses with the truth that is in themselves" (*Confessions* X.6). We can have access to God's message
only by looking into ourselves and reading this truth in our souls.
Armed with the knowledge of truth in ourselves, we can then turn
back to the world and read it. This reading process, however, requires constant movement back and forth in comparing the message the world gives with "the truth that is in [ourselves]."

Any reading of God's text, however, involves a rational statement about God's message, and the reading will necessarily misrepresent the truth it seeks: "even those who are most gifted with
speech cannot find words to describe you" (*Confessions* I.4). "Have
we spoken or announced anything worthy of God? Rather I feel
that I have done nothing but wish to speak: if I have spoken, I
have not said what I wished to say. Whence do I know this, except
because God is ineffable? If what I said were ineffable, it would
not be said. And for this reason God should not be said to be ineffable, for when this is said something is said. And a contradiction
in terms is created, since if that is ineffable which cannot be
spoken, then that is not ineffable which can be called ineffable"
(*On Christian Doctrine* I.6). When Saint Augustine tries to attribute
a particular quality to God, such as ineffability, his statement suggests its opposite. The very act of calling God ineffable undermines
itself, for it suggests that God cannot be completely ineffable if
he can be called ineffable. Even a negative statement is wrong,
for God cannot even be called ineffable.

Nevertheless, despite our inability to represent God as the message of the universe, we are continually motivated to persist in
our search to read his truth: "The thought of you stirs him so
deeply that he cannot be content unless he praises you, because
you made us for yourself and our hearts find no peace until they
rest in you" (*Confessions* I.1). Indeed, for Augustine, rational statements, although erroneous, do serve a useful function in the pursuit of God's truth. They must continually undermine themselves
by revealing their inadequacy in order to suggest God negatively;
God can only be where language is not, for no human representation can capture him adequately.[2] Similarly, the mystical tradition
in general holds that in order to gain access to God, the mind must

be stripped of every concept and imagination, of all pretenses to knowledge and understanding.[3] In this way Augustine believed that we will be forced to look within ourselves, in particular to our memory, the ultimate place of knowledge. True understanding "is recognized by us in our minds, without images, as they actually are. . . . [In this] process of thought . . . we gather together things which although they are muddled and confused, are already contained in the memory" (*Confessions* X.10). "For I found my God, who is Truth itself, where I found truth. . . . So, since the time when I first learned of you, you have always been present in my memory, and it is there that I find you whenever I am reminded of you and find delight in you" (X.23). True knowledge and faith come about through a radical forgetting of our conventional notions about the world and God so that we can open up to the pre-rational memory of God, which cannot be codified.[4]

Because God has always been present inside the human memory, which can have a knowledge of things divine without recourse to representation, Augustine did not link the problem of faith to that of representation. The problems of representing God or the world did not put God's existence in question. For Pascal, however, who was in the Cartesian world, radically different from Augustine's world, the problem of representation was catapulted to the center of consciousness, as it was for the seventeenth century in general.[5] As *res cogitans* was separated from *res extensa,* the main concern was to know how the former could represent the latter. Pascal questioned how we could know whether our memory can represent our past life with God. For him, it was not clear whether memory can transcend representation or whether it is caught within its structures. Our inability to represent God may point either to his hidden nature, the punishment for our corruption, or to the complete absence of such a divine Being. As noted in chapter 3, we have no way of knowing rationally whether the "secret instinct" from our first nature represents a former paradise or former human constructs of paradise: "I am very much afraid that nature itself is only a first custom, just as custom is a second nature" ("J'ai grand peur que cette nature ne soit elle-même qu'une première coutume, comme la coutume est une seconde nature" [S159, L126, B93]).

## READING, REPRESENTATION, AND THE PRISON
## OF HUMAN CONSCIOUSNESS

In order to explore the question of representation, and ultimately that of faith, Pascal, like Augustine, asks us to look within to see how we read, that is, how we represent the world and ourselves: "the order of thought is to begin with oneself" ("l'ordre de la pensée est de commencer par soi" [S513, L620, B146]). But what we find by looking inward is not a universal Cartesian "natural light" or a primordial memory that directly links us to God. Rather, what we discover is the apparent absence of such a faculty, which would help us to know the truth rationally. Or if such knowledge does, in fact, exist, it is just as hidden as the Pascalian God and the author of the *Pensées*.

What we discover by turning inward is the absence of a unified consciousness lying at the origin of our existence. The lack of a unified consciousness subverts the traditional notion of reading, for it questions the autonomy of author and reader. For Pascal, the "I" who writes and reads a text is already him or herself a conglomerate of other texts. Authors are not the originators of their words; they inhabit a language whose signifying system predates them: "I have used old words" ("je me suis servi des mots anciens" [S575, L696, B22]). Because the linguistic and thought structure is borrowed, texts can generate borrowed meanings not intended by the authors. The authors then always intend only a fragment of the total possible meanings that their texts engender. Indeed, the Pascalian text suggests that authors are not the sole origin of what they write:

> Some authors, speaking of their words, say: "My book, my commentary, my history," and so on. They resemble middle-class people who have houses of their own and always have "my house" on their tongues. They would do better to say: "Our book, our commentary, our history," and so on, because there is in them usually more of other people's than of their own.

> Certains auteurs, parlant de leurs ouvrages, disent: "Mon livre, mon commentaire, mon histoire, etc." Ils sentent leur bourgeois qui ont pignon sur rue, et toujours un "chez moi" à la bouche. Ils feraient mieux de dire: "Notre livre, notre commentaire, notre histoire, etc.," vu que d'ordinaire il y a plus en cela du bien d'autrui que du leur [B43].[6]

The shift from "my" to "our" or "other people's" suggests it is the communal aspect of language which undermines authorial sovereignty. On the literal level, authors do control their writing: they decide to take up a pen at a particular moment and intend to say specific things. If one were to view the writing process as operating simply in one direction, from authors to texts to readers, as Descartes would have it, one could regard authors as the originators of their writing. The writing process is reversible, however: the language and the reader also write the text because language is the common property of the community's shared codes. As suggested in my analysis of the Port-Royal *Logique* (see chap. 1), when the words leave the authors' minds to find existence on the written page, they undergo a separation that makes them free to evoke unintended meanings contained in the linguistic system and in the minds of the readers.

The "I" that writes the text is not the author of him or herself but is written by the desires and decisions of others. The unity of consciousness is dissolved, for its capacity as desirer or decision maker and meaning maker is taken over by a series of systems that operate through it:

> Custom makes masons, soldiers, roofers. "He is an excellent roofer," they say, and, speaking of soldiers, "They are quite crazy," whereas others, on the contrary, say: "There is nothing as great as war; everyone else is worthless." From hearing people praise these occupations in our childhood and putting down all the others, we make our choice. For we naturally love virtue and hate folly; the very words will decide; we go wrong only in applying them.

> La coutume fait les maçons, soldats, couvreurs. C'est un excellent couvreur, dit-on, et en parlant des soldats: ils sont bien fous, dit-on, et les autres au contraire: il n'y a rien de grand que la guerre, le reste des hommes sont des coquins. A force d'ouïr louer en l'enfance ces métiers et mépriser tous les autres on choisit. Car naturellement on aime la vertu et on hait la folie; ces mots mêmes décideront; on ne pêche qu'en l'application [S527, L634, B97].

One's desire to be a mason or a soldier does not spring spontaneously from the inner core of one's being; rather, it comes from observing and imitating, perhaps unconsciously, the desires of others. Our desires are determined by their conscription in a system of opinions, customs, languages, over which they have no control. Instead of the individual's shaping the system, the system creates the individual by molding its desires and decision-making processes according to its needs.

For this reason, the self, as either source or object of a text, is always a product of language. All we have are signs of the self and, as in any text, their interpretation is uncertain.

> "What is the self?" . . .
>
> And if someone loves me for my judgment or my memory, do they love me? *Me*, myself? No, for I could lose these qualities without losing myself. Where then is this self, if it is neither in the body nor in the soul? And how can one love the body or the soul except for the sake of such qualities, which are not what make up the self, since they are perishable? Would we love the substance of a person's soul, in the abstract, whatever qualities might be in it? That is not possible, and it would be wrong. Therefore we never love anyone, but only qualities. . . . we never love anyone except for borrowed qualities.

> Qu'est-ce que le moi? . . .
>
> Et si on m'aime pour mon jugement, pour ma mémoire, m'aime-t-on? *moi*? Non, car je puis perdre ces qualités sans me perdre moi-même. Où est donc ce *moi*, s'il n'est ni dans le corps, ni dans l'âme? et comment aimer le corps ou l'âme, sinon pour ces qualités, qui ne sont point ce qui fait le moi, puisqu'elles sont périssables? car aimerait-on la substance de l'âme d'une personne, abstraitement, et quelques qualités qui y fussent? Cela ne se peut, et serait injuste. On n'aime donc jamais personne, mais seulement des qualités. . . . on n'aime personne que pour des qualités empruntées [S567, L688, B323; italics in original].

Although the "borrowed qualities" are not synonymous with an essential self, if indeed it exists, they are the only qualities that one can seize upon and thus they serve as the representations, the signs, of the self. For this reason authors, like God, are hidden from consciousness. "Where then is this *self*?" All we have is a text, a collection of signs, qualities that are borrowed, but no integral self. As borrowed selves having borrowed desires and writing in borrowed linguistic and semantic structures, authors are cut off from an understanding of themselves as well as from their texts and readers.

Whereas the sign systems that operate through the "I" who writes a text undermine his authorship, the sign systems that operate through the "I" who reads the text temporarily grant him authorship. Readers read by way of culturally inherited sign systems that distort their consciousness both of themselves and of the outer world and texts.[7] In fact, readers rewrite the world by projecting their culturally inherited sign system onto it. For example, the outer world, because of the double infinite and its hidden author, does not present itself as a preexisting text. If we wish to read it to find God's truth, we must first represent it to ourselves; we must write the world as text. The reader writes the text by deciding what shape it should assume. But the readers' text of the world can never coincide with the world itself, as its hidden Author probably knows it. Describing the disproportion between humankind and the double infinity of the world, the narrator writes:

> . . . let him see the earth as a mere speck compared with the vast orbit described by this star, and let him marvel at finding this vast orbit itself to be no more than the tiniest point compared with that described by the stars revolving in the firmament. . . . The whole visible world is only an imperceptible dot in nature's ample bosom. No idea comes near it; it is in vain that we inflate our conceptions beyond imaginable space, for we bring forth only atoms compared with the reality of things.

> . . . que la terre lui paraisse comme un point au prix du vaste tour que cet astre décrit, et qu'il s'étonne de ce que ce vaste tour lui-même n'est qu'une pointe très délicate à l'égard de celui que les astres qui roulent dans le firmament embrassent. . . . Tout le monde visible n'est qu'un trait imperceptible dans l'ample sein de la nature. Nulle idée n'en approche, nous avons beau enfler nos conceptions au-delà des espaces imaginables, nous n'enfantons que des atomes au prix de la réalité des choses [S230, L199, B72].

All we have are human representations that we project onto the real world, and we can have no definite knowledge of anything that lies beyond them: "Instead of receiving ideas of these things in their purity, we color them with our qualities and stamp our own composite being on all the simple things we contemplate" ("Au lieu de recevoir les idées de ces choses pures, nous les teignons de nos qualités et empreignons notre être composé de toutes les choses simples que nous contemplons" [S230, L199, B72]). We are truly trapped in language and we cannot transcend it to know whether we are writing only our own text or God's text. If we are locked in a self-enclosed universe where all reading fails to locate an objective text or truth but merely rewrites texts in accord with our shifting conventional structures, how, then, can we read? Pascal asks us to read our rewritings of the world, our representations. In fact, Pascal is less interested in the world that we do represent than in the way we attempt to represent it, equate it with truth, and then discover its fragmentary nature, its falsity. Our readings alternate between our belief, on the one hand, that we have captured the truth and, on the other hand, our realization that our truths are merely a function of our projected conventions. This pattern of reading corresponds to the greatness and misery of humankind. Human greatness consists in projection and rewriting, in the ability to create order out of chaos: "Man's greatness even in his concupiscence is such that he has managed to produce an admirable system from it" ("Grandeur de l'homme dans sa concupiscence même, d'en avoir su tirer un réglement admirable" [S150, L118, B402]). Moreover, the greatness of humans also lies, in part, in the fact that they do not equate their codes with truth but perceive them simply as codes, which makes them desire to look beyond codes. That these codes, however, are but mere signs of order, and do not correspond to the truth itself, signals human misery. Readers are miserable because all their attempts to read, to impose a rational order on texts, degenerate into mere signs of truth that reflect back on their own structures of reading: "The greatness of man is great in that he knows himself to be miserable; a tree does not know itself to be miserable. One is thus miserable to know that one is miserable, but there is greatness in knowing that one is miserable" ("La grandeur de l'homme est grande en ce qu'il se connaît misérable; un arbre ne se connaît pas misérable. C'est donc être misérable que de [se] connaître misérable, mais c'est être grand que de connaître qu'on est misérable" [S146, L114, B397]).

Pascal asks us to look within to see how this form of reading corresponds to the dual structure of our debased consciousness: "Observe yourself and see if you do not find the living proof of [your greatness and misery]" ("Observez-vous vous-mêmes et voyez si vous n'y trouverez pas les caractères vivants de [votre grandeur et misère]" [S182, L149, B430]). "For is it not clearer than day that we feel within ourselves the indelible marks of excellence, and is it not equally true that we constantly experience the effects of our deplorable condition?" ("Car n'est-il pas plus clair que le jour que nous sentons en nous-mêmes des caractères ineffaçables d'excellence et n'est-il pas aussi véritable que nous éprouvons à toute heure les effets de notre déplorable condition" [S240, L208, B435]).

The *Pensées* stimulate a form of reading that swings back and forth between the greatness of thinking one has discovered the true reading and the misery of knowing that this reading is merely the product of a conventional structure we impose upon it. The *Pensées* privilege this form of reading because it makes us aware that we are cut off from reality. It contrasts with the rationalist form of reading which seeks to repress such an awareness by creating the impression that signs correspond to truth. Awareness of our imprisonment in culturally inherited sign systems comes only when our attempts to read the world rationally fail. We then realize that our notions of truth and of the outer world are but projections of our conventional sign systems: "It is in vain that we inflate our conceptions beyond imaginable space, for we bring forth only atoms compared with the reality of things. Nature is an infinite sphere whose center is everywhere and whose circumference is nowhere" ("[N]ous avons beau enfler nos conceptions au-delà des espaces imaginables, nous n'enfantons que des atomes au prix de la réalité des choses. C'est une sphère infinie dont le centre est partout, la circonférence nulle part" [S230, L199, B72]).[8] To understand "the reality of things" we project certain forms, such as the circle, onto it, but these forms are incapable of capturing it. Reality lies beyond human constructs: "no ideas come near it" (S230, L199, B72).

In our attempt to read the world, we discover that what we view as reality is only a representation that does not mirror reality but reflects back on our semiological codes: "A city, a countryside, from afar is a city or a countryside, but as one approaches, it becomes houses, trees, tiles, leaves, grass, ants, ants' legs, and so on ad infinitum. All that is included in the word 'countryside'"

("Une ville, une campagne, de loin c'est une ville et une campagne, mais à mesure qu'on s'approche, ce sont des maisons, des arbres, des tuiles, des feuilles, des herbes, des fourmis, des jambes de fourmis, à l'infini. Tout cela s'enveloppe sous le nom de campagne" [S99, L65, B115]). From one perspective, the word *campagne* seems to be an accurate representation of reality. But when we change perspectives, we realize that we have only an arbitrary sign of reality. Despite the constant flight of reality from our representations of it, we have no choice but to continue projecting structures onto it with the hope that we will someday arrive at an unmediated vision of reality. In the process of searching, however, we become aware that our readings of the world are simply projections of our preconceived notions: "What else can he do then, but *perceive some semblance of the middle* of things, in an eternal despair of knowing either their principles or their end?" ("Que fera(-t-)il donc sinon *d'apercevoir quelque apparence du milieu* des choses dans un désespoir éternel de connaître ni leur principe ni leur fin" [S230, L199, B72; emphasis added]). Although the positing of a "middle" is a fiction, it is a necessary one to make sense of a limitless world. The fixed point need not necessarily assume the form of a middle; it can also be either an end point or a beginning point:

> Thus we see that all the sciences are infinite in the range of their research, for who can doubt that geometry, for instance, has an infinite infinity of propositions to expound? They are infinite also in the multiplicity and subtlety of their principles, for anyone can see that those that are supposed to be ultimate do not stand by themselves but depend on others, which depend on others again, and thus never allow of any finality.
>
> But *we treat as ultimate* those that seem so to our reason, as in material things *we call a point indivisible* when our senses can perceive nothing beyond it, although by its nature it is infinitely divisible.

> C'est ainsi que nous voyons que toutes les sciences sont infinies en l'étendue de leur recherches, car qui doute que la géométrie par exemple a une infinité d'infinités de propositions à exposer. Elles sont aussi infinies dans la multitude et la délicatesse de leurs principes, car qui ne voit que ceux qu'on propose pour les derniers ne se soutiennent pas d'eux-mêmes et qu'ils sont appuyés sur d'autres qui en ayant d'autres pour appui ne souffrent jamais de dernier.

> Mais *nous faisons des derniers* qui paraissent à la raison, comme
> on fait dans les choses matérielles où *nous appelons un point indivisible,*
> celui au-delà duquel nos sens n'aperçoivent plus rien, quoique
> divisible infiniment et par sa nature [S230, L199, B72; emphasis
> added].

Unable to find a true middle or end, we must construct models
of a structure based on our habitual associations of signs. We
then project these configurations onto the world before us and
call them meaning. We realize that our interpretive constructs
are only constructs, however, when they fail to correspond to
reality. It is this very disjunction between representation of reality
and reality itself which forces us to reread our text. We then
realize that what we blindly called the outer world is only a text.
Our awareness of this projection also allows us to discover that
the signs and structures with which we construct this text come
from the culturally inherited sign systems that constitute our
modes of perception. In this way we become aware that all reading
requires the projection of an inner system of signs onto an outer
world, which we transform into a text. We are thus entrapped in
the solipsistic text we write, which is always other than the world
it represents.

## READING THROUGH THE "I": DESCARTES— READER OF SAINT AUGUSTINE; PASCAL— READER OF MONTAIGNE

Pascal presents Descartes as an example of one type of reader who
unconsciously reads through the mediation of his own private
sign system. In his unfinished essay, "On the Art of Persuasion,"
Pascal discusses Descartes as a reader of Saint Augustine. Pascal
notes that Descartes, in reading Augustine's text, transforms it
and attempts to make it his own. He does not seek to repeat the
text in its original form but rewrites it according to the rational
part of his representational system:

> I would like to ask equitable persons if this principle—"Mat-
> ter is in a state of being naturally and irremediably incapable of
> thought"—and this one—"I think, therefore I am"—are in effect

the same thing in Descartes' mind as they are in the mind of Saint
Augustine, who said the same thing twelve centuries earlier.

In truth, I am far from saying that Descartes is not the true
author of these statements, even if he had only read them in the
writings of this great saint.

Je voudrais demander à des personnes équitables si ce principe:
"La matière est dans une incapacité naturelle, invincible de penser," et celui-ci: "Je pense, donc je suis", sont en effet une même
chose dans l'esprit de Descartes et dans l'esprit de saint Augustin,
qui a dit la même chose douze cents ans auparavant.

En vérité, je suis bien éloigné de dire que Descartes n'en soit
pas le véritable auteur, quand même il ne l'aurait appris que dans
la lecture de ce grand saint."[9]

Descartes' reading of Saint Augustine focused on specific grammatical statements: "Matter is in a state of being naturally and
irremediably incapable of thought" and "I think, therefore I am."
Guided by his rational, inner structures, Descartes appropriated
these statements from Saint Augustine in such a way that they
have become the major principles of his thought. Pascal argues
that Descartes should be viewed as if he were their author, even
though he "learned" them through reading Saint Augustine. What
makes Descartes an author and not a plagiarist is the fact that
his appropriation springs from the projection of a part of his own
conceptual framework, a rational part, onto Augustine's text, in an
attempt to integrate Augustine's words and statements into his
own system and thus make them his own.[10] Pascal notes that the
meaning of these statements cannot be controlled by the person
who articulates them. The meaning of Saint Augustine's sentences
cannot be fixed by their grammar, for they are subject to transformation. They have one meaning in the context of Augustine's
thought and a very different meaning in Descartes' system. "Those
who have discriminating minds know that there is a world of difference between two similar words, depending on the places and circumstances in which they are used" ("Ceux qui ont l'esprit de dis-
cernement savent combien il y a de différence entre deux mots sem-
blables, selon les lieux et les circonstances qui les accompagent").[11]

That is not to say, however, that Descartes' appropriation of
Saint Augustine allows him to possess the latter's thought and

erect himself as permanent author. Appropriation inevitably gives way to disappropriation because Descartes, the newly transformed reader/author, after rewriting the text, finds himself in the same position as his predecessor. He, too, will be disappropriated by his discourse, by language that writes his discourse. Reading, in this way, releases reader and author from any strict control or faithfulness to each other. Interpreting the words according to one's own representational system implies that readers disown the author as source, since the words rooted in the reader may grow in directions unintended by the author: "The same thoughts grow sometimes differently in another mind than in the one of their author; infertile in their natural ground, they become fruitful when transplanted" ("Les mêmes pensées poussent quelquefois tout autrement dans un autre que dans leur auteur: infertiles dans leur champ naturel, abondantes étant transplantées").[12] Descartes transplants a part of Saint Augustine's text into the fertile ground of his own mind to arrive at a better understanding of his own thought. He reads Augustine in order to read his own way of representing the world. This notion of reading as appropriation and rewriting rather than as repetition threatens the control of the classical and rationalist model by bringing out the hidden violence of reading. Paradoxically, the only way to arrive at the author's intention is to leave it temporarily, to seek within oneself the means of integrating the author's text. To appropriate someone else's thought, however, is to displace it, and readers cannot be certain that their reading corresponds to the one intended by the author. Such appropriation is continually subjected to disappropriation by yet other readers; no author or reader is ever the master of his or her discourse.

In referring to himself as a reader of Montaigne, Pascal indirectly comments on the reading process as projection, rewriting, and appropriation/disappropriation: "It is not in Montaigne but rather in myself that I find everything I see in it" ("Ce n'est pas dans Montaigne mais dans moi que je trouve tout ce que j'y vois" [S568, L689, B64]). The reading of this fragment, or of any text, is rendered problematic by the absence of any contextual statements and by the potentially dangerous rhetorical structure inherent in language which gives rise to alternative grammatically correct statements. The readers' interpretation of this fragment depends on the reference of "it." On the one hand, if "it" refers to Montaigne's text, the fragment may suggest that everything Pascal finds in the Montaigne text is simply a projection of what he sees in himself. In reading Montaigne, he projects his own structures onto fragments of the whole work, rewrites them according to his own system of thought, and appropriates them, thus suggesting that he is only reading himself. On the other hand, if the "it" refers to Pascal's own view of the world, one may interpret the fragment as a denial of Montaigne's influence on his own text, a declaration of independence from the father-text that Pascal was accused of plagiarizing. Although Pascal may aspire to separate himself from his predecessor, it does not follow that his reading of the world can in fact be independent, for all readings are determined by the duality of the human condition, greatness and misery, which leads him to set up and break down semiological codes. As with the Montaigne text, Pascal must use his culturally inherited sign system to rewrite and appropriate the world. And thus in reading the world he will be reading himself.

What may seem to be a declaration of independence in the second reading, however, is expressed in terms that evoke dependence. It turns out that Pascal borrowed the syntactic structure of this fragment from the very person from/with whom he wishes to disentangle/entangle himself. His fragment clearly echoes Montaigne: "It is neither in Plato nor in myself, since he and I understand and see things the same way" ("Ce n'est non plus selon Platon, que selon moi: puisque lui et moi l'entendons et voyons de même" [*Essais*, I, 26]). Pascal has grafted many of Montaigne's syntactic structures, as well as his ideas, onto his own text. The Sellier edition of the *Pensées* illustrates the extent to which Pascal rewrote the *Essais* by carefully citing in footnotes the passages borrowed from Montaigne. The borrowings are so extensive and detailed that one must conclude, as does Bernard Croquette, that Pascal often wrote the *Pensées* with the Montaigne text next to him and copied sentences out of it, sometimes changing only a few words or expressions.[13]

This dependence on Montaigne's text brings out yet a third meaning of Pascal's fragment. Montaigne places the text cited above in the following context: "Truth and reason are common to everyone; they do not belong either to the person who stated them first or to the one who repeated them. It is neither in Plato nor in myself, since he and I understand and see things the same way" ("La vérité et la raison sont communes à chacun, et ne sont non plus à qui les a dit premièrement, qu'à qui les dit après. Ce n'est non plus selon Platon que selon moi: puisque lui et moi l'entendons et voyons de même"). Montaigne, as reader of Plato, seems to be denying the notion of authorship by claiming that certain truths are common to all and the same for all and that therefore they cannot be owned by any individual who happens to articulate them. Although Pascal also denies the notion of authorship, he does so for an opposite reason: truth is intransmissible. Thus Pascal rewrites Montaigne's text in order to make an opposite point. And in so doing he demonstrates that we never discover anything but our own ideas, even in another's writings. Pascal shows that the same statement placed in two different contexts— the Montaignian and Pascalian texts—suggests different meanings.

Although Pascal's reading and rewriting of Montaigne may appear to violate the integrity of the *Essais*, his so doing seems to bring him close to Montaigne rather than to create a rift between them, for Montaigne encourages the appropriation of texts: "I would like someone who would know how to pluck the feathers off me" ("J'aimerais quelqu'un qui me sache déplumer"). He also writes (I, 25):

> We store the opinions and knowledge of others and that is all. We must make them ours. We resemble someone needing fire who goes to a neighbor's house, stops to warm up, and, upon finding such a beautiful blaze there, forgets to bring it home. What is the point of having a stomach full of meat if we cannot digest it? If it does not change form in us? If it does not increase and fortify us?

True understanding requires that we rewrite previous texts and attempt to make them our own.

Pascal does not go so far as to claim that the readers are always and necessarily cut off from the author. Projection may lead the readers to capture the author's spirit and central meaning, or it may lead them onto diverging paths. However, just as fallen humans can never know if they have seized upon the truth of God the Author, so too can fallen readers never know with certainty that they have grasped the author's intended meaning.

## READING THROUGH THE "I": THE HISTORY OF THE *PENSÉES'* EDITIONS/READINGS

Readers of Pascal's text have in fact, although perhaps reluctantly, or unknowingly, read it in the manner in which it asks to be read: through projection and rewriting. This form of reading, however, was necessitated by the unusual and chaotic state of the manuscript when it was found. That chaotic state emphasizes the notion of the *Pensées* as a fallen text and reminds us that all attempts to arrive at a truth are hindered by our fallen nature. As is well known, the *Pensées* are fragments ranging from developed thoughts to random jottings found in a state of semiordered chaos after Pascal's death. Although Pascal had classified many of them into twenty-eight titled *liasses,* approximately 60 percent of them remained unclassified. In order to read this disordered text, one has no choice but to project a unity onto it and rewrite it. Bereft of clear signs from Pascal concerning his intentions, Etienne Périer, Pascal's nephew and one of his earliest editors, as well as all subsequent editors and readers of the *Pensées,* was in a position curiously similar to that of the readers dramatized in the *Pensées* who seek to read the world. Just as the fallen Pascalian reader is described as separated from God's voice, so too the editor/reader is separated from Pascal's voice. They are all faced with the infinite in which the author falls silent, left with few guidelines to order, organize, and find meaning in their respective texts. The editors/readers of the *Pensées,* confronted with the eternal silence of Pascal, a God-like figure who alone could orient their reading, resemble the fallen individual who "in looking at the whole mute universe" ("en regardant tout l'univers muet") discovers that he is "without light, left to himself" ("sans lumière abandonné à lui-même" [S229, L198, B693]).

The experience of reading the *Pensées* thus recreates the central drama it describes: the story of the desire for truth, an "objective" text, and the inability to satisfy this desire. But because an objective text escapes us, we must reflect upon its very possibility. We become aware that reading is an activity that can never escape the filter of our perceptual and conceptual modes which enclose us in our own fallen universe. The editorial history of the readers' response to the *Pensées* supports the notion that all reading involves projection and rewriting. Deprived of any absolute truth or guidelines, the readers/editors must fall back on their culturally inherited sign systems to construct an order and impose it on the *Pensées*. And that is precisely what Etienne Périer and the Port-Royal committee decided to do in the first edition of the *Pensées*. Yet they denied that they were imposing an order on the *Pensées*. They claimed to be presenting Pascal's thoughts "as they were found, without adding or changing anything" ("telles qu'on les a trouvées, sans y rien ajouter ni changer").[14] Moreover, they said they had decided not to "add in any way to the work [M. Pascal] had aimed to produce" ("suppléer en quelque sorte l'ouvrage que [M. Pascal] voulait faire"), since any such edition would be misleading. Despite their protestations to the contrary, Périer and the Port-Royal committee finally selected only fragments that were clear and complete (incompletion being synonymous with imperfection), arranging them "in a somewhat orderly fashion presenting the fragments on the same topics under the same headings" ("dans quelque sorte d'ordre sous les mêmes titres que celles qui étaient sur le même sujet").[15] Despite their belief that they were being faithful to Pascal, Périer and the committee members nevertheless projected their own order onto the *Pensées* and rewrote the text. They "corrected" some of the fragments to prevent the criticism of fideism and attenuated Pascal's hostility toward Cartesianism. Moreover, their system of classification took little heed of the ordering of the fragments in their respective liasses but grouped them under thirty-two titles that were basically of their own invention. Furthermore, they altered Pascal's style to suit the Port-Royal conventions of eloquence. While professing fidelity to Pascal's thought, they interpreted it as mirroring their own.

All subsequent editors/readers disappropriated the old constructions of the text and projected different unities onto the amorphous mass of notes that lay before them. They rewrote and reappropriated them according to their own culturally inherited systems of signs. The Port-Royal's arrangement of the fragments according to content set a precedent for the editions that came out in the next two centuries, each successive edition "completing" or arranging the *Pensées* to reflect their own values. For example, Condorcet's edition (1776) appeals to the Age of Enlightenment. His selection and grouping of the fragments emphasizes Pascal's skepticism and intimates a latent atheism.

In the early nineteenth century Victor Cousin addressed the

French Academy to demonstrate the inadequacies of the Port-Royal text, on which existing editions had been based. Essentially, he pointed out that what one had interpreted as an "objective" text was but the projection of the Port-Royal editors' preconceived notions. Cousin established the foundation for new projections and rewritings of the text. He suggested that editors look to internal and external evidence of a plan rather than try to decipher a unity based on the content.[16] Editors thus vied with one another to remedy the "subjective" vagaries of the text and to reproduce the most reliable outline of Pascal's intended apology. Editions proliferated, each one proposing to penetrate the innermost reaches of Pascal's thought by discovering his true plan. Faugère (1844) asserted that he had uncovered "the author's plan," Astié (1857), "a new plan," Rocher (1873), "the author's only true plan," Jeannin (1883), "the author's plan," Vialard (1886), "Pascal and the Apologists' plan," Michaut (1896), "the original outline," and Didot (1886), "the author's desired order." Although these editors presented utterly different texts, they were all based on the original manuscript (MS 9202).[17]

The old interpretive code upon which editions were based was once again dismantled and replaced by the research findings of Louis Lafuma.[18] Lafuma demonstrated the insufficiency of the original manuscript, upon which most previous editions had been based, and proved the superiority of the copy (MS 9203). Lafuma revolutionized Pascalian scholarship by noting that the fragments were partly classified into *liasses* and by observing that the copy reproduced that classification. He based his analysis on Etienne Périer's account: "We found them all together, tied in various bundles but lacking order and continuity. . . . The first thing we did was to have them copied as they were, and in the same confusion in which they were found" ("On les trouva tous ensemble enfilés en diverses liasses, mais sans aucun ordre et aucune suite. . . . La première chose que l'on fit fut de les faire copier tels qu'ils étaient, et dans la même confusion qu'on les avait trouvés"). Lafuma concluded that this copy was the key to Pascal's true order and meaning.[19]

Philippe Sellier, however, pointed out a serious shortcoming of the interpretive code upon which the Lafuma edition was based.[20] Sellier's edition, like all good editions, gives unity to the text. To render the text more clear and better ordered, in the unclassified section Sellier added his own titles, such as "The Discourse of the Machine," "Letter Leading to the Search for God," and "Discourse of Corruption." His titles, which seem to be perfectly justified, illustrate the necessity of projecting our own forms of unity onto a text so that it can "speak" to us. Nevertheless, the fact that each edition requires the projection of a meaning does not imply that all editions are equal. Some projections are better grounded in the text than others. The essential point is that no edition can ever capture the totality of this infinitely open text.

The process by which one projects unity onto the *Pensées* and rewrites them helps us to understand that reading is a fall from the text as a secure paradise of truth with a God-like author. The readers thus fall into a labyrinth of misreadings. One may view the attempts made in successive editions to order the signs of the *Pensées* and arrive at the truth of the text as another reenactment of the story of the fall from the illusion of truth (discussed in chap. 3). Each edition gives the impression that its codes correspond to the truth; each one creates the illusion that its editor has discovered the definitive order and the most comprehensive reading. Then, however, another edition introduces a different order based on a different code which shows how the preceding one had blindly fallen into error and given rise to inaccurate and incomplete readings. Each new edition falls into the pride of assuming that human signs contain truth, and thus proposes a new order and a new unity which it believes to hold the secret to the text's meaning. But it is this very process of creating and breaking down the text which constitutes the essential reading experience. It is only by reflecting on the pursuit of truth that one realizes that truth is trapped in the hermeneutic circle.

The editors' effort to reconstruct an order is inevitably caught in the hermeneutic circle. The editors have approached the reconstruction of the *Pensées* from two opposing angles. Some of them chose to arrange the fragments on the basis of their content, first hypothesizing a model of the whole and then proceeding to order the parts in accordance with that model. Others chose to arrange the fragments on the basis of the parts represented in the copy of the manuscript. They deduced the meaning of the whole through the ordering of the parts. The proper place of a part cannot, however, be evaluated without an understanding of the whole—and we do not have the whole, only a model of the whole. To decide upon the particular order of the fragments within each liasse, to decide which fragments were destined to be included in the *Pensées* or to be chosen for another work, requires a broader comprehension of the work. Conversely, a comprehension of the whole can be deduced only from its parts (whose status can be determined only in relation to the whole)—and all we have is a representation of the parts. The editors are inevitably caught in the paradoxical relation of the part to the whole. This hermeneutic circle, wherein the whole must be deduced from a representation of the parts, and the parts must be deduced from a model of the whole, is described by Pascal in order to question the possibility of ever arriving at an objective meaning:

> Thus, since all things are both caused or causing, assisted and assisting, mediate and immediate, providing mutual support in a chain linking together naturally and imperceptibly the most distant and different things, I consider it as impossible to know the parts without knowing the whole as to know the whole without knowing the individual parts.

> Donc toutes choses étant causées et causantes, aidées et aidantes, médiates et immédiates et toutes s'entretenant par un lien naturel et insensible qui lie les plus éloignées et les plus différentes, je tiens impossible de connaître les parties sans connaître le tout, non plus que de connaître le tout sans connaître particulièrement les parties [S230, L199, B72].

All we can have is a facsimile of the text. The process of constructing the text itself highlights the extent to which it is a function of our preconceived notions. If, as Pascal suggests, a total, objective meaning cannot be reached, why should his text be accorded a different status? Can it escape the very problems that it articulates? Editors, as real readers of the *Pensées*, are caught in the same hermeneutic bind that the *Pensées* describe as constituting the major roadblock to a transcendent truth.

In opposition to readers who believe that the only way to understand the *Pensées* is to piece together Pascal's fragments by taking scissors to paper, other readers elevate the fragment to the stature of a new form. For Goldmann, the fragment is the only adequate form of expression for Pascal's paradoxical text. It is "complete only by its incompleteness" ("achevé de par son inachèvement"). To look for the true plan of the *Pensées* thus seems to Goldmann to be an "antipascalian enterprise par excellence, an enterprise that goes against the coherence of the text and implicitly fails to recognize what constitutes both its intellectual content and the essence of its literary value."[21] In keeping with this discursive order or, more precisely, disorder, Marin has defined the fragment as the appropriate form of the *Pensées:* "The problem of the text in Pascal and in the *Pensées* is a key problem: the *Pensées* constitute a sort of text-laboratory that permits the production of a text to be tested against its form which is the fragment, against its discursive mode which is interruption, and against its own logic which is digression. . . . The meaning of the Pascalian text, understood as the plurality or possibility of meaning, is its discontinuity."[22]

The "dis-order" and discontinuity created by the fragmentary nature of the text are sanctioned by the Bible. Sellier and Stanton argue that Pascal's perception of the style and order of Scripture determined the writing of his own work:[23]

Order. Against the objection that Scripture has no order.

The heart has its order, the mind has its own, which is by principle and demonstration.

The heart has another . . .

Jesus Christ and Saint Paul have the order of charity, not of the mind, for they wish to warm, not to instruct . . .

The same with Saint Augustine. This order consists principally in digressions on each point that relates to the end, to show the dominance of this end.

L'ordre. Contre l'objection que l'Ecriture n'a pas d'ordre.

Le coeur a son ordre, l'esprit a le sien qui est par principe et démonstration.

Le coeur en a un autre . . .

J.C. Saint Paul ont l'ordre de la charité, non de l'esprit, car ils voulaient [échauffer], non instruire . . .

Saint Augustin de même. Cet ordre consiste principalement à la digression sur chaque point qui a rapport à la fin, pour la montrer toujours [S329, L298, B283].

The digressive order of the heart (or charity) characterizes biblical discourse and constitutes the model for Pascal's writing. Stanton elucidates the digressive order of Scripture by arguing that it "re-presents" the "ultimate discontinuity of the metaphysical order."[24] She maintains that the metaphysical order in Pascal's text (the "order of God, or God as order")[25] is based on a logic that is radically different from the one that controls human communication. The metaphysical order embraces opposing verities, whereas human logic refuses them (S614, L733, B862). The seemingly contradictory truths of the metaphysical order produce a "dis-orderly dialectic" which "constitutes the mode of thought of the order of charity and, like God's chiaroscuro, (over)-determines the disposition of Pascal's text."[26]

The value of disorderly fragments in the human order of Pascal's text lies in the fact that they invite, yet thwart, the readers' effort to project a unity onto them and rewrite them. Many indications within the text solicit the construction of a possible order: "Part (1). Misery of man without God. Part (2). Happiness of man with God." ("(1). Partie. Misère de l'homme sans Dieu. (2). Partie. Félicité de l'homme avec Dieu" [S40, L6, B60]). "This is where the chapter on the powers of deception must start" ("Il faut commencer par là le chapitre des puissances trompeuses" [S78, L45, B83]). "A letter on the folly of human knowledge and philosophy. This letter to be put before the section on diversion" ("Une lettre de la folie de la science humaine et de la philosophie. Cette lettre avant le divertissement" [S27, L408, B74]). These internal indices, as well as the existence of textual gaps, entice the readers to insert themselves in the interstices. And, in fact, many readers have responded in such a fashion. The *Pensées* have inspired well over 150 editions, each one seeking to establish the text by proposing a different order and reading. Yet no edition has been able to give a definitive reading.

Although the problem of order is essential to the *Pensées*, the truth of the text is not to be found either in yet another edition that purports to have discovered the original order intended by Pascal or in the notion of a disordered, fragmentary text as a new form. The *Pensées* are a machine that invites and breaks down the illusion that they have a unity; they are a machine that crushes the prideful belief that they can be rationally controlled. By encouraging and undermining our belief that the order of the text is true, the *Pensées* force us to recognize that no unifying order can exist on the human plane. They thus compel us to look outside the text, outside language, for a hidden order to unify the contradictory readings. The hidden order and unity can lie neither in a new edition nor in a different arrangement of its signs, for no sign can say directly what it means. Whatever the hidden order and unity are, they can never be stated.

## A NEW MODEL OF READING

The notion of reading as projection and rewriting at first seems to be negative, because it suggests that a radical rift separates readers from the original text. Such a separation would lead one to question the value of reading. But, in fact, the goal of reading for Pascal is not to transmit a truth that can be contained in language; indeed, language cannot contain a truth. Rather, the text seeks to create the conditions by which the readers come to experience language's inability to represent truth as the essence of their fallen nature. As noted in chapter 3, the goal for each set of signs, faith's story of the Fall and Redemption or uncertainty's story of a fall from the illusion of truth, is to throw us into an opposite system of signs so we realize that truth lies in no text. Our very failure to grasp the text's original meaning turns us back on the process by which we continually rewrite the text. The awareness of reading as rewriting and as misrepresentation underscores our distance from truth. The *Pensées'* narrator suggests a mode of interpretation whereby the consciousness of distance from truth initiates a new level of meaning: "In writing down my thought it escapes me sometimes, but that reminds me of my weakness, which I am always forgetting, and it teaches me as much as my forgotten thought, for I care only about knowing my nothingness" ("En écrivant ma pensée elle m'échappe quelquefois; cela me fait souvenir de ma faiblesse que j'oublie à toute heure, ce qui m'instruit autant que ma pensée oubliée, car je ne tiens qu'à connaître mon néant" [S540, L656, B372]). Because of memory slips, the writer forgets the main object of his thought. Although his lapse blocks out the original thought, it creates the condition for the emergence of a second level, one that focuses on his subjective process. The forgetting of his thought makes him experience his forgetfulness, his weakness. The intellectual content or objective meaning has less impact than the direct experience of his weakness or nothingness as it is manifested through the difficulty of reading and seizing his thought.

The *Pensées* dramatize the problem of reading in order to help us find a new model of reading, one that transforms obstacles to an objective meaning into a different level of meaning that focuses on the subjective process of reading and writing oneself. This second level of meaning involves the realization that one is always being written by someone else. One of the key factors making us realize that we are always being written by someone else is the obscurity of texts when we seek to read them according to the traditional, rationalist model. The constant refrain of rationalist readers who attempt to read God's truth in the world is, "What must I do? I see nothing but obscurities" ("Que dois-je faire. Je ne vois partout qu'obscurités" [S38, L2, B227]). For Pascal, however, obscurity actually proves its truthfulness, instead of creating terror and constituting an obstacle to Christianity: "Recognize then the truth of religion in its very obscurity" ("Reconnaissez donc la vérité de la religion dans l'obscurité même de la religion" [S690, L439, B565]). The obscurity of the world does not reflect outward upon the objective existence of truth or of God but reflects back on the confused subject's situation. It reflects back on our corruption and on our fallen state: "What are we to conclude from all our obscurities if not our unworthiness?" ("Que conclurons-nous de toutes nos obscurités, sinon notre indignité?" [S690, L445, B558]). In a displacement of the interpretive framework, Pascal turns obscurity around so that it does not suggest the absence of divine truth but rather our fall from it, our corruption. Obscurity opens us up to religion, not through explaining a content that will appeal to our intellect, but by constituting a blockade against our traditional modes of knowing.

Pascal transforms obscurity into figures that point to themselves as language or, more precisely, as fallen language. But by figuring themselves as false, as fallen into error, they also figure the possibility of a truth that can only be elsewhere and written only by someone else. If there is a truth, it cannot be stated but only figured, because the truth is always other than what language states and the author intends. Signs can never represent directly what they mean. Although one may continually try to capture the truth through signs, the pursuit will be endless because the truth will always be where language is not. This, however, does not mean that we cannot know the truth of the Pascalian text or of God. It just means that we cannot read the truth *in* a text; we cannot have certain *rational* knowledge of it because Pascal's rational statements point not only to one grammatical meaning but also to their opposite, which is also true. Linguistic statements will always be in error. The truth, then, must exist outside language, outside the *Pensées*. But language is a necessary means of attaining the truth of its limits, even if it cannot contain a transcendent truth.

Given my statement of the limitations inherent in *any* attempt to arrive at the "correct meaning" of a text, it is necessary to comment on the status of my own reading. My reading, like all readings, is a misreading. Mine, however, differs from most in that it accounts for itself as a misreading. I propose a reading and then show how it undermines itself and throws us into an opposite reading, which also undermines itself. My goal, then, is to describe the way the text moves back and forth between misreadings. In so doing, I am interested in meaning not as a *product* buried in the text but as an *act* of reading—of projection and rewriting. I focus on the mind as it is engaged in the process of seeking truth and failing to find it. A "correct" reading must understand how and why it will always be incorrect.

## CHRIST AS MODEL READER: READING THE HIDDEN ORDER AND THE HIDDEN AUTHOR

If we know how our signs misfunction, we will not attempt to read God with the semiological codes that condition us to look to an outside text, expecting to find a secret meaning buried there. God's meaning does not lie in any text or in any rational reading. It lies in a feeling in the heart which is atextual. It is only by understanding the futility of human semiological systems, the absurdity of rational readings, that we can open ourselves up to the fact that God can write us and the texts that we project onto the

world. God writes us by projecting his light onto us through our
hearts. Only when guided by the unity of light that God projects
onto us can we project a unity onto the world. If reading involves
the projection of an illuminated inner system of signs onto an
outer text that we rewrite, the only way to embrace a unity is to
allow God's unity to read and rewrite the world through us.

Christ is a model of how we should read; only Christ knew that
God writes through him. In *Writings on Grace*, Pascal writes: "Jesus
Christ himself said . . . 'It is not I who creates these works, but the
Father who is in me,' and yet he says elsewhere: 'The works that
I have created.' Jesus Christ is not a liar, and his humility has
not injured his truth. One can thus say, since he said it, that he
has created some works and he has not created them" ("Jésus-
Christ dit lui-même . . . 'Ce n'est pas moi qui fais les oeuvres, mais
le Père qui est en moi,' et néanmoins il dit ailleurs: 'Les oeuvres
que j'ai faites' (Jn, xiv, 10, 12). Jésus-Christ n'est point menteur,
et son humilité n'a point fait tort à sa vérité. On peut donc dire,
puisqu'il l'a dit, qu'il a fait des oeuvres et qu'il ne les a pas
faites").[27] In the perspective of grace, Christ's statements are not
contradictory; Christ recognizes the duality of his nature. He is
responsible for his thoughts and acts and yet he accepts that God
writes through him.

God communicates with humans through Jesus Christ; God has
Christ live in humans as God lives in Jesus Christ: "Saint Paul
says: 'I live, not I, but Jesus Christ lives in me'" ("Saint Paul dit:
'Je vis, non pas moi, mais Jésus-Christ vit en moi' (Gal. II, 20)").[28]
Through the heart, the hidden Author, God, can rewrite the readers' conventional sign systems and read through them, projecting
his light onto them through Jesus Christ. True understanding
comes from rewriting them in the correct manner: by projecting
onto them our consciousness that God has rewritten through
Christ. It is only when their consciousness is authored by God's
unity that readers can feel the unity of any text: "Those who believe
without having read the Testaments do so because their inward
disposition is truly holy and what they understand about our religion conforms to it. They feel that a God made them. They want
only to love God; they want only to hate themselves" ("Ceux qui
croient sans avoir lu les Testaments c'est parce qu'ils ont une disposition intérieure toute sainte et que ce qu'ils entendent dire de

notre religion y est conforme. Ils sentent qu'un Dieu les a faits. Ils ne veulent aimer que Dieu, ils ne veulent haïr qu'eux-mêmes" [S413, L381, B286]). God communicates with humans, not by presenting them with signs in the outer world, but by acting as a hidden author who can be the secret author of the sign system that they project onto the world. The world becomes a text written by God through Christ only for the elect reader who knows how to rewrite it, how to transform it into a text, by projecting onto it a sign system authored by God who illuminates the reader through the heart: "*Knowledge of God*. Those whom we see to be Christians without knowledge of the prophecies and proofs are no less sound judges than those who possess such knowledge. They judge with their hearts as others judge with their minds. It is God himself who inclines them to believe and thus they are most effectively convinced" ("*Connaissance de Dieu*. Ceux que nous voyons Chrétiens sans la connaissance des prophéties et des preuves ne laissent pas d'en juger aussi bien que ceux qui ont cette connaissance. Ils en jugent par le coeur comme les autres en jugent par l'esprit. C'est Dieu lui-même qui les incline à croire et ainsi ils sont très efficacement persuadés" [S414, L382, B287]).

The prison of our culturally inherited sign system with which we represent the world is essential to Pascal's conception of reading because it alone reminds us that truth can come only from the heart, which transcends the "prison-house of language." The heart, the seat of the most fundamental knowledge, can apprehend its truths outside language, "And it is on such knowledge, coming from the heart and instinct, that reason must depend and base all its discourse" ("Et c'est sur ces connaissances du coeur et de l'instinct qu'il faut que la raison s'appuie et qu'elle y fonde tout son discours" [S142, L110, B282]). Because understanding provided by the heart may come from God and escape textuality, which is always in error, it alone is persuasive, whereas knowledge communicated by reason is falsified by its signs: "And that is why those to whom God has given religious faith by moving their hearts are very fortunate and feel quite legitimately convinced, but to those who do not have it we can give such faith only through reasoning, until God gives it by moving their hearts, without which faith is only human and useless for salvation" ("Et c'est pourquoi ceux à qui Dieu a donné la religion par sentiment de coeur sont bien heureux et bien légitimement persuadés, mais ceux qui ne l'ont pas nous ne pouvons la [leur] donner que par raisonnement, en attendant que Dieu la leur donne par sentiment de coeur, sans quoi la foi n'est qu'humaine, et inutile pour le salut" [S142, L110, B282]). Through the heart the readers can give Pascal's text something it cannot contain: a unity, an author.

Pride and the desire for rational control are the major obstacles to the form of reading the *Pensées* propose, for humans do not want to think that someone else reads them, writes them, speaks them, acts them. Prideful humans do not want to give up what they perceive as rational control and be creatures through whom God reads, speaks, acts. Yet to open one's heart to God, Pascal argues, is not to give up rational control, but only the belief in it, for rational control is only an illusion. In asking us to allow God to read us, we are not giving up very much, Pascal argues, because something other always speaks us, reads us, writes us, and acts us. Without God, this "something other" is the language that structures human meaning. The signs of self are trapped in the discourse of the body, which mechanically determines one's habits of thought, desire, reading. By dint of repetition, these habits appear to be natural and to stem from spontaneous desire because we forget their conventional origins. Pascal wants the readers to fall from the illusion that their codes correspond to the outer world: they serve only a purely conventional text that is necessarily fallen into the hermeneutic circle. Then, instead of being authored by this circle, they can leave themselves open to being authored by God's light which can, through the heart, transform our conventional representational structures and the way we read the outer world.

Although language can never directly state the truth of Pascal's text or of God, we can perhaps come to know the hidden order and unity of both, which exist outside human language, by understanding how our signs misrepresent truth. It is only by searching and failing to find order and truth through our readings that we reflect back on language as obstacle. When we realize that we are trapped in language, the hermeneutic circle, our signs become figures that point not only back to themselves but also beyond themselves to a truth that can only exist elsewhere. But the readers can never find that "elsewhere" as long as they remain in language. Pascal asks us to make a wager that we can transcend language and open up our hearts to allow God, rather than language, to read through us. By trying to give up everything, our language, we may gain everything, God. Of course, we have no way of knowing rationally whether the force that is authoring us is actually God or just the hermeneutic circle. This knowledge is not available to reason or to language. We remain caught in the aporia in which neither God's presence nor his absence can be proven. Only the heart can pretend to transcend what our reason can never resolve.

# Conclusion

Because, according to Pascal, we are fallen from the knowledge of truth into language, all our statements about the human condition, God, and the fall itself are trapped in figures that always say something other than what they appear to say. Rhetoric replaces epistemology; instead of knowledge of God or truth, we have figures of God or truth. Nevertheless, the fall into language breeds the desire to escape. We seek to discover whether these unpredictable figures might not follow some indirect and cryptic course that leads to an ultimate point of reference: God or a transcendent truth. However, our efforts to escape language and gain access to truth do not succeed. As the language in which we are trapped is a fallen language, the metalanguage with which we represent to ourselves our attempts to transcend language is also fallen. Language can produce only incompatible stories about where our interpretations of figures lead. According to one story, told from the perspective of faith, our interpretation of figures ultimately transcends language and discloses a truth; according to the other, told from the perspective of uncertainty, interpretation discloses only the signs with which it produces a notion of God. Neither of these stories is completely true, nor is either of them totally false: each story is caught between truth and falsity. They culminate, however, in radically contradictory interpretations of interpretation. They fall into an aporia which implies that all epistemological statements are products of mere stories of how we interpret signs. Narrative thus replaces epistemology. Instead of truth, we have stories of how to decode signs and produce representations of truth and God.

If truth is replaced by signs of truth, if we are in a world of figures and stories instead of a world of true or false statements about God, then how can we gain access to the truth of God? Although we are trapped in a fallen language where truth can only be other than what it says or implies, this fallen language is, paradoxically, the only tool available to help us approach an understanding of God. Our only hope lies in the possibility that the otherness that marks our fallen discourse is ultimately a figure of God's otherness.

The Pascalian God, if he exists, is characterized by his difference from humankind, his complete otherness, for he is hidden from human modes of representation. "If there is a God, he is infinitely incomprehensible since, being indivisible and limitless, he bears no relation to us. We are thus incapable of knowing either what he is or if he is. This being the case, who will dare try to resolve this question? Not we, who have no affinity with him" ("S'il y a un Dieu, il est infiniment incompréhensible, puisque, n'ayant ni parties ni bornes, il n'a nul rapport à nous. Nous sommes donc incapables de connaître ni ce qu'il est, ni s'il est. Cela étant, qui osera entreprendre de résoudre cette question? Ce n'est pas nous, qui n'avons aucun rapport à lui" [S680, L418, B233]). The truth of God, if such a truth exists, is irrevocably other than what we say about him: "The things of God [are] inexpressible" ("Les choses de Dieu [sont] inexprimables" [S303, L272, B687]). Only "God speaks well about God" ("Dieu parle bien de Dieu" [S334, L303, B799]).

The inexpressibility of God means that we cannot directly communicate his possible truth; we can only say that our signs fail to represent him adequately. This negative form of representation harks back to the tradition of negative theology. The otherness of the Pascalian God, however, is more radical than the God described by this tradition and with which his God must be compared. According to the *via negativa*, God's otherness, the very fact that we cannot describe him, ultimately points not to his absence but to his existence; the fact that God escapes language is a sign of his superiority. Negative theology, then, presupposes that at the end of the series of negative statements regarding our representations of God lies the ultimate affirmation of God.

For Pascal, however, no such affirmation can be certain, as it would presuppose that one can escape the hermeneutic circle created by language. Moreover, as scientist and philosopher, as well as theologian, Pascal cannot ignore the logical implications of the negative thrust of negative theology's method of argument. For Pascal, the inability of human language to represent God's otherness does not point to God's superiority. Rather, it points to the structure of language itself with its rational aporia which continually holds out the illusory promise that the full truth will ultimately be revealed in the otherness of an alternative story.

Indeed, the aporia of the *Pensées* is constituted by an otherness that tosses us back and forth between opposing fictional stories. Our search for the truth that this otherness promises causes us to move back and forth between opposing sides of an aporia, with the hope that the other side of the aporia possesses the truth that is excluded from the present one. Readers of the *Pensées* have continually tried to negate the effects of the text's otherness by affirming one side of this aporia. They have posited an ultimate truth that lies at the end of its continual series of negations but, in so doing, they have repressed a part of the text. No truth is sufficient to account for the entirety of the text; a recalcitrant otherness inevitably asserts itself in our attempt to read the *Pensées*. Trapped in the aporia between two opposing stories, the truth exists only as an extrapolation from language's ability to point to, but not to prove, the existence of what it is not.

Given the otherness of God and of human discourse, the traditional notion that Pascal wrote an apology is indeed problematic. An apology implies the direct communication of an intended meaning, and Pascal's theory of language clearly shows such a communication to be a highly questionable notion. Nonetheless, there is strong evidence to suggest that Pascal bets on the possibility that his text can communicate something. What he communicates is clearly not a logical truth about God's existence, for such a truth would be caught in the infinite bind of an aporetic discourse. Rather, borrowing partly from the tradition of negative theology, he communicates the impossibility of communicating; he makes the readers read the impossibility of reading his text. Each reading seeks to represent the totality of a text's truth. But as soon as the interpretive framework of a given reading fails to account for the more obscure regions of a text, as soon as it en-

counters an otherness that resists penetration, the reading is forced
to reflect back on itself. In this autoreflexive moment it will perceive itself as a misrepresentation. The text thus engages the readers in a process of reading their own representations which reveal
themselves as misrepresentations. By pulling the readers into the
vortex of an endless process of reading how they necessarily mis-
construe the text, the *Pensées* make them aware of the otherness
of all discourse. This otherness is situated within the linguistic
realm itself. Unlike negative theology, however, the *Pensées* leave
it to the reader to decide if it constitutes a metaphor for divine
otherness, an unreadable resemblance to the otherness of God.
Such a resemblance would be unreadable since it can have no
basis in logic. Unlike negative theology, Pascal thus seems to
wager that once the readers realize the impossibility of reading,
they will discover a resemblance between the text's otherness and
an otherness outside the realm of logic—one they feel in their
hearts, one that will lead them to God.

# Notes

## Introduction

1. Friedrich Nietzsche, *Gesammelte Werke* (Munich: Musarion Verlag, 1922–1929), XXI:89. For a detailed comparative study of Pascal and Nietzsche, see Elise Lohmann, *Pascal und Nietzsche* (Leipzig: Druck von Robert Naske, 1917); James Dionne, *Pascal et Nietzsche: étude historique et comparée* (New York: Burt Franklin, 1965); Charles Natoli, *Nietzsche and Pascal on Christianity* (New York: Peter Lang, 1985).

2. Within the traditional view of the relationship between language and knowledge of God, there are two distinct currents: the rational and the nonrational. According to Rudolf Otto (*The Idea of the Holy: An Inquiry into the Non-Rational Factor in the Idea of the Divine and Its Relation to the Rational* [London: Oxford University Press, 1957]), the rational current posits that God's attributes constitute clear and definite concepts. They can be grasped by the intellect, analyzed by thought, and expressed in language. The nonrational current tends toward a mystical understanding of God. In this perspective, God is ineffable and he eludes our conceptual way of understanding; God defies our linguistic categories. The fact that language is not capable of capturing God's essence, however, does not mean that absolutely nothing can be asserted of the object of religious consciousness. If no assertions were possible, mysticism would exist only in unbroken silence. And the mystics have certainly not been silent; they are generally characterized by their abundant eloquence. Ultimately, they believe that the heart can transcend language to feel the inexpressible mystery above all creatures. According to both the rational and nonrational approaches to God, then, one can get beyond language to arrive at a transcendent truth.

3. Fredric Jameson, in *The Prison-House of Language* (Princeton: Princeton University Press, 1972), shows how modern critical theory derives from the awareness that we are imprisoned in signs.

4. For a discussion of the paradoxical nature of Pascal's thought, see Lucien Goldmann, *Le Dieu caché: Etude sur la vision tragique dans les Pensées*

*de Pascal et dans le théâtre de Racine* (Paris: Gallimard, 1959), and Robert Nelson, *Pascal: Adversary and Advocate* (Cambridge: Harvard University Press, 1981).

5. Blaise Pascal, *Pensées,* ed. Philippe Sellier (Paris: Mercure de France, 1976), fragment 313; ed. Louis Lafuma (Paris: Intégrale, 1963), fragment 281; ed. Léon Brunschvicg (Paris: Hachette, 1964), fragment 613. Hereafter only the fragment numbers from these three editions, in the order here cited, are given. The translations are my own.

6. Pascal's insistence on the Fall and on a hidden God clearly aligns him with Saint Augustine. For a comparison of their theological doctrines, see Philippe Sellier, *Pascal et Saint Augustin* (Paris: Colin, 1970).

7. Edouard Morot-Sir, in *La Métaphysique de Pascal* (Paris: PUF, 1973), argues that all questions of knowledge must be situated within a linguistic universe.

8. Certainly the problem of expressing the otherness of a God who lies outside the ken of human knowledge is by no means new to Pascal. It has commonly been discussed in religious philosophy ever since Philo (see Harry Wolfson, *Studies in the History of Philosophy and Religion* [Cambridge: Harvard University Press, 1973]) and lies at the root of many contemporary discussions of religious discourse (see Karl Barth, *Church Dogmatics* [Edinburgh: T & T Clark, 1975; Dietrich Bonhoeffer, *Creation and Temptation* [London: SCM Press, 1966], and *Ethics* [New York: Macmillan, 1955]). Historically, this problem has been posed most strongly in connection with negative theology, which holds that nothing positive can be known about God, who has nothing in common with any other being. No predicate or descriptive term may rightfully be attributed to him unless it is given a meaning that is wholly different from the one the term has in common usage and is purely negative. All statements concerning God considered in himself should, if they are to be regarded as true, be interpreted as providing an indication of what God is *not.* In his *Guide to the Perplexed,* Maimonides writes: "Know that the description of God . . . by means of negations is the correct description—a description that is not affected by an indulgence in facile language and does not imply any deficiency with respect to God." In the fourth century Hilary of Poitiers summarized what was commonly viewed as the orthodox belief of the early Church: "There can be no comparison between God and earthly things. . . . We must therefore regard any comparison as helpful to man rather than as descriptive of God, since it suggests rather than exhausts the sense we seek. . . . Neither the speech of man, nor the analogy of human nature can give us a full insight into the things of God. The ineffable cannot submit to the bounds and limitations of definition" (De Trin. vii.7). Saint Augustine writes that we cannot even describe God

as ineffable, for if "what I said were ineffable, it would not be said. And for this reason God should not be said to be ineffable, for when this is said something is said. And a contradiction in terms is created, since if that is ineffable which cannot be spoken, then that is not ineffable which can be called ineffable" (*On Christian Doctrine*, I, 6).

The belief that language is inadequate to express God's truth stems largely from religious awe, a reverential abstinence from the use of God's name (see Ian Ramsey, *Words about God* [London: SCM Press, 1971]). Theologians thus adopted a *via negativa*, an approach suggesting that God can best be described in negatives to protect him from the imperfections of human modes of knowledge and expression (see Vladimir Lossky, *Théologie négative et connaissance de Dieu chez Maître Eckhart* [Paris: Vrin, 1960]). But, for Pascal, unlike his predecessors, the inability of human language to express directly God's truth results less from reverential awe and more from the fear of God's distance or separation from the world. Pascal's negative theology arises from his awareness of the negative impact of the Fall on human thought and discourse.

9. Surprisingly, the Fall has received little attention among readers of Pascal. David Wetsel, in *L'Ecriture et le reste: The Pensées of Pascal in the Exegetical Tradition of Port-Royal* (Columbus: Ohio State University Press, 1981), addresses the question the most directly by arguing that Pascal seeks to prove the historical truth of the Fall and Redemption.

10. See Louis Marin, *La Critique du discours* (Paris: Minuit, 1975), "'Pascal': Text, Author, Discourse . . . ," *Yale French Studies* 52 (1975): 129–151, and *On the Interpretation of Ordinary Language: A Parable of Pascal,*" in *Textual Strategies: Perspectives in Post-Structuralist Criticism*, ed. Josué V. Harari (Ithaca: Cornell University Press, 1979). Marin seeks to show that there are incompatible logics at work within the Pascalian text.

11. It may seem surprising to refer to the *Pensées* as a story because the scholarly tradition has tended to view them as a discourse of philosophic and religious truth. It is my contention, however, that stories, signs, and narrative must replace truth and epistemology in the Pascalian fallen world. (For discussion of this question see chap. 3, esp. n. 1.)

12. I am accepting the name "Pascal" only as a conventional sign of the author. Indeed, the relationship between Pascal as author and the "I" of the text is problematic (see chap. 3, pp. 105–108). Louis Marin puts the word Pascal in quotation marks (see "'Pascal'") and analyzes the complexities of the relation between the author and the "I" who is speaking in the text. Domna Stanton uses the term "inscribed author" to refer to the textualized author (see "Pascal's Fragmentary Thoughts: Dis-Order and Its Overdetermination," *Semiotica* 51 [1984]:211–235). Although these approaches are appropriate, I have chosen to use the more

conventional designation of Pascal for the major speaking voice. Although one has no way of knowing with certainty that the speaking "I" of the text is Pascal, one also has no way of knowing with certainty that it is not.

13. See Hugh Davidson, *The Origins of Certainty: Means and Meaning in Pascal's Pensées* (Chicago: University of Chicago Press, 1979); Henri Gouhier, *Blaise Pascal: Commentaires* (Paris: Vrin, 1966); Thomas Harrington, *Vérité et Méthode dans les Pensées de Pascal* (Paris: Vrin, 1972); Jean Mesnard, *Les Pensées de Pascal* (Paris: SEDES, 1976); Jan Miel, *Pascal and Theology* (Baltimore: Johns Hopkins University Press, 1969); Anthony Pugh, *The Composition of Pascal's Apologia* (Toronto: University of Toronto Press, 1984); Sellier, *Pascal et Saint Augustin* and *Pascal et la liturgie* (Paris: PUF, 1966); Wetsel, *L'Ecriture et le reste*.

14. See Jean-Jacques Demorest, *Dans Pascal: Essai en partant de son style* (Paris: Minuit, 1953), and *Pascal Ecrivain: Etude sur les variantes de ses écrits* (Paris: Minuit, 1957); Lucien Goldmann, *Le Dieu caché;* Dom Jungo, *Le Vocabulaire de Pascal* (Paris: D'Artrey, 1950); Michel Le Guern, *L'Image dans l'oeuvre de Pascal* (Paris: Colin, 1969); Sister Mary Louise Maggioni, *The Pensées of Pascal: A Study in Baroque Style* (Washington: Catholic University Press, 1950); Patricia Topliss, *The Rhetoric of Pascal: A Study of His Art of Persuasion in the Provinciales and the Pensées* (Leicester: Leicester University Press, 1966).

15. Edouard Morot-Sir, "Du Nouveau sur Pascal?" *Romance Notes* 18(1972):272–279.

16. Ibid., p. 277.

17. Ibid., p. 278.

18. See Julien-Eymard d'Angers, *L'Apologétique en France de 1550 à 1670: Pascal et ses précurseurs* (Paris: Nouvelles Editions Latines, 1954), pp. 29–50.

19. The underpinnings of these incompatible logics are present in both elements in Christianity's heritage, Scripture and Hellenistic philosophy. Scripture repeatedly suggests that God is wholly incommensurable with his creation and stresses the hidden nature of God, *Vere tu es Deus absconditus* (Isa. 45:15). To be the God of the Bible, he must be utterly different from all finite created beings. And yet, despite God's Otherness, the Bible combines graphic images depicting things divine with fairly explicit statements on the Deity's purposes and emotions. Some genuine knowledge of God must exist if he has been revealed to humankind. Statements about God cannot be totally unintelligible. Similarly, in Hellenistic philosophy, the Supreme Being is assumed to be completely simple, immutable, and thus fundamentally above our fragmentary concepts. At the same time, however, this Being is the ultimate source of all intelligibility and, as a result, constitutes the unique knowable reality.

Theologians have sought to resolve this conflict by recourse to argument by analogy. According to James Ross ("Analogy and the Resolution of Some Cognitivity Problems," *Journal of Philosophy* 67 [1970]:725–746), the analogical theory, extensively developed by Saint Thomas Aquinas, was designed to provide a *via media* between two conflicting views of religious discourse: the anthropomorphic doctrine of univocal predication and the negative theology of equivocal predication. In the former, the predicates we positively attribute to God mean the same thing when attributed to him as when attributed to ordinary creatures. In the latter, the predicates we positively attribute to God mean something entirely different from what they mean when they are attributed to other creatures, since God is wholly other. Aquinas rejects both views and claims that the predicates, when applied to God, have a meaning analogous to the meaning they have when applied to ordinary things. (See Baruch Brody, *Readings in the Philosophy of Religion: An Analytic Approach* [Englewood Cliffs: Prentice-Hall, 1974].) Ross and Brody argue that the analogy doctrine informs contemporary efforts to reconcile the two incompatible logics.

Pascal rejects such efforts to bring together what he perceives as two irreconcilable logics; he denies the force of reason that lies at the heart of the Thomistic attempt to resolve the conflict between univocal predication and equivocal predication.

20. Pascal's implicit attack on the decidability of reason is an attack on the pride of the rationalists who set out to prove the truth of Christian dogma directly by natural reason. In *The Rhetoric of Pascal*, Topliss characterizes Christian apologetics as following two opposing traditions, optimistic rationalism and pessimistic Augustinianism, situating Pascal clearly in the latter. Optimistic rationalists such as Silhon and Yves de Paris believe that the existence of God and the possibility of Redemption can be demonstrated by rational proof, whereas the pessimistic Augustinians believe that one can make only indirect, negative affirmations about God's existence. All human activity bears the mark of Original Sin, even the attempt to know God.

21. Jacques Derrida, "Structure, Sign and Play," in *Structuralist Controversy*, ed. Richard Macksey and Eugenio Donato (Baltimore: Johns Hopkins University Press, 1970), p. 264.

## 1: Seventeenth-Century Discourse: Sin and Signs

1. See Pierre Kuentz, "Le 'rhétorique' ou la mise à l'écart," *Communications* 16 (1970):143–157.

2. J.-F. Sénault, *L'Homme criminel*, 4th ed. (Paris, 1656), p. 274. He also writes: "Eloquence is the work of sin; men have sought out figures only to camouflage their lies, and they have developed eloquence when

they became criminal. Innocence would not have spoken this language, and if the Holy Scripture uses it on occasion, I imagine that it is to adapt itself to human usage and to imitate the goodness of God, which assumes our passions when it deals with us" (ibid., p. 267).

3. "Le dogme chrétien fournit cet écart originel qui permet de poser, d'un seul mouvement, l'écart et la négation de l'écart. Il postule, en effet, fondement de la démarche rhétorique, une transgression initiale, un faux-pas fondateur, un décalage originaire" (Kuentz, "Le 'rhétorique,'" p. 153).

4. Jacques Derrida, *Of Grammatology*, trans. Gayatri Chakravorty Spivak (Baltimore: Johns Hopkins University Press, 1976), p. 283.

5. See Hugh Davidson, *Audience, Words, and Art: Studies in Seventeenth-Century French Rhetoric* (Columbus: Ohio State University Press, 1965).

6. The concept of classicism and its relation to seventeenth-century thought is somewhat problematic. Until recently it has been customary to view the seventeenth century as dominated by classical thought, which places a premium on the universal science of order. In *The Order of Things* (New York: Vintage, 1973), Michel Foucault writes that in the classical age "the ordering of things by means of signs constitutes all empirical forms of knowledge" (p. 57). He also says that classical language has strong confidence in the representative capacity of linguistic signs. For a developed discussion of the traditional view of classicism, see Jules Brody, ed., *French Classicism: A Critical Miscellany* (Englewood Cliffs: Prentice-Hall, 1966).

Jules Brody and Domna Stanton have pointed out to me, however, that the traditional notions of classicism are conventional constructs and do not accurately reflect the complexity of seventeenth-century literature. Stanton specifically takes issue with Foucault's notion of *le langage classique* of the seventeenth century in her article, "Playing with Signs: The Discourse of Molière's *Dom Juan*," in *French Forum* 5 (1980):106–121. Although I certainly agree that "classicism" is a simplistic label, the concept does, nevertheless, provide a useful heuristic device to allow the analysis of a complex problem without getting lost in all the modifications that would be necessary to render thought as precisely as possible.

7. René Descartes, *Discourse on Method*, trans. F. E. Sutcliffe (New York: Penguin, 1968), p. 78.

8. René Descartes, *Lettre à Mersenne* (Nov. 20, 1629), in *Oeuvres complètes* (Paris: Pléiade, 1937), p. 702.

9. Ibid.

10. Timothy J. Reiss, "The Word/World Equation," *Yale French Studies* 49 (1973):8.

11. Descartes, Réponse à la 4$^{\text{ième}}$ objection de Hobbes.

12. A number of poststructuralist studies of Descartes show how the Cartesian semiological system undercuts itself. See Timothy Reiss, "The 'concevoir' Motif in Descartes," in *La Cohérence Intérieure: études sur la littérature française du XVII<sup>e</sup> siècle* (Paris: J. M. Place, 1977), pp. 203–222, and "Cartesian Discourse and Classical Ideology," *Diacritics* (Winter 1976): 19–27; Sylvie Romanowski, *L'Illusion chez Descartes: La Structure du discours cartésien* (Paris: Klincksieck, 1974).

13. For a study of the history of rhetoric, see Roland Barthes, "L'Ancienne Rhétorique," *Communications* 16 (1970):172–229.

14. Kuentz, "Le 'rhétorique,'" p. 147.

15. See Davidson, *Audience, Words, and Art*, pp. 3–85. See also Kuentz, "Le 'rhétorique'". Walter J. Ong, *Ramus: Method and the Decay of Dialog* (Cambridge: Harvard University Press, 1958).

16. Barthes, "L'Ancienne Rhétorique," pp. 175–176.

17. Plato, *The Gorgias*, 449a–458c.

18. Plato, *The Phaedrus*, 267b.

19. Paul Ricoeur, *La Métaphore vive* (Paris: Seuil, 1975), p. 18.

20. Descartes, *Discourse on Method*, p. 84.

21. C. F. de Vaugelas, *Remarques sur la langue française utiles à ceux qui veulent bien parler et bien écrire* (Paris: Baudry, 1880), pp. 577–578.

22. D. Bouhours, *Les Entretiens d'Ariste et d'Eugène* (Paris: Cluny, 1962), p. 108.

23. D. Bouhours, *La Manière de bien penser dans les ouvrages d'esprit* (Paris, 1688), p. 12.

24. Vaugelas, *Remarques*, p. 593.

25. Bouhours, *Les Entretiens*, p. 75.

26. Bouhours, *La Manière*, p. 28.

27. Ibid., p. 22.

28. Bouhours, *Les Entretiens*, p. 77.

29. Bouhours, *La Manière*, p. 31.

30. Ibid.

31. See Louis Marin, *La Critique du discours* (Paris: Minuit, 1975), who analyzes these tensions at work in *La Logique*.

32. Antoine Arnauld and Pierre Nicole, *La Logique ou l'art de penser* (Paris: Flammarion, 1970), p. 50.

33. Ibid., p. 130.

34. Ibid.

35. Ibid.

36. Ibid., p. 194.

37. Ibid., p. 195.

38. Ibid.

39. Ibid.

40. Ibid., p. 194.

41. For development of this problem in Pascal's *Pensées*, see my article, "Pascal's *Pensées*: Economy and the Interpretation of Fragments," *Stanford French Review* 6 (1982): 207–220.

42. Arnauld and Nicole, *La Logique*, p. 196.

43. Ibid., p. 95.

44. Noam Chomsky (*Language and Mind* [New York: Harcourt Brace Jovanovich, 1972]) finds in the Port-Royal *Logic* and *Grammar* a predecessor for his theory of transformational grammar. In the Port-Royal theory he discovers the notion of a surface structure and a deep structure and the transformations that allow us to pass from one to the other: "The deep structure is related to the surface structure by certain mental operations—in modern terminology, by grammatical transformations. . . . Following the Port-Royal theory to its logical conclusions, then, the grammar of language must contain a system of rules that characterizes deep and surface structures and the transformational relation between them. . . . the speaker makes infinite use of finite means. His grammar must, then, contain a finite system of rules that generates infinitely many deep and surface structures, appropriately related" (p. 17). See also Chomsky's *Cartesian Linguistics: A Chapter in the History of Rationalist Thought* (New York: Harper and Row, 1966), which also develops the relation of his notion of transformational grammar to the Port-Royal theory.

45. Arnauld and Nicole, *La Logique*, p. 127.

46. Ibid., p. 136.

47. Ibid., p. 137.

48. Ibid., p. 130.

49. Ibid., p. 196.

50. Ibid., pp. 132–133.

51. In *Le Coeur et la raison selon Pascal* (Paris: Elzévir, 1950) and in *La Doctrine de la Grâce chez Arnauld* (Paris: PUF, 1922), Jean Laporte, for example, minimizes many crucial differences among the Jansenists.

52. Lucien Goldmann, *Le Dieu caché: Etude sur la vision tragique dans les Pensées de Pascal et dans le théâtre de Racine* (Paris: Gallimard, 1959), and Goldmann, ed., *Correspondance de Martin de Barcos* (Paris: PUF, 1956), p. 47.

53. According to Goldmann, Henri Bremond, who wrote the famous *Histoire littéraire du sentiment religieux*, claimed not to have even read Barcos.

54. Goldmann, *Correspondance de Barcos*, p. 240.

55. Ibid., p. 135, Lettre à la Mère Angélique (18 June 1652).

56. Ibid., p. 290, Lettre probablement à M. de Saci (18 July 1659).

57. Ibid., pp. 373–374, Lettre à M. de Saci (13 Jan. 1669).

58. For another analysis of this fragment, see Marin, *La Critique du discours*.

# NOTES TO PAGES 38–48

155

59. There are, however, other fragments that question this perspective. I discuss the complexities of this issue in chapter 3.

## 2: The Fall from Truth into Language

1. See Patricia Topliss, *The Rhetoric of Pascal: A Study of His Art of Persuasion in the Provinciales and the Pensées* (Leicester: Leicester University Press, 1966).

2. For a full discussion of the hermeneutic circle, see Hans-Georg Gadamer, *Philosophical Hermeneutics*, trans. and ed. David E. Linge (Berkeley, Los Angeles, London: University of California Press, 1976). See also the issue of *New Literary History* on literary hermeneutics, 10 (1978).

3. Plato, *The Meno*, 81C.

4. For a discussion of Plato's doctrine of recollection see Jacob Klein, *A Commentary on Plato's Meno* (Chapel Hill: University of North Carolina Press, 1965), pp. 115–135.

5. For a discussion of the relationship between Pascal and Saint Augustine, see Philippe Sellier, *Pascal et Saint Augustin* (Paris: Colin, 1970).

6. For a discussion of this doctrine, see Hugh Davidson, *The Origins of Certainty: Means and Meanings in Pascal's Pensées* (Chicago: University of Chicago Press, 1979); Thomas Harrington, *Vérité et Méthode dans les Pensées de Pascal* (Paris: Vrin, 1972); A. W. S. Baird, *Studies in Pascal's Ethics* (The Hague: Martinus Nijhoff, 1975).

7. For an analysis of Plato's divided line, see Allan Bloom's interpretive essay and the notes to his translation of *The Republic* (New York: Basic Books, 1968).

8. Although the centrality of Pascal's doctrine of the three orders has been widely discussed, only one study, to my knowledge, has attempted to show how it actually functions in Pascal's text. Hugh Davidson, in *The Origins of Certainty*, argues that the three orders provide interpretive frameworks that clarify the shifting meaning of important words and concepts in the *Pensées:* "The same words (as for example, 'éclat,' 'grandeur,' 'victoire') take on different meanings or references . . . as the center of attention shifts up and down the series of orders. . . . Love, once bad, as concupiscence, is transformed into charity; the mind, once proud and hostile, humbles itself in the wager; the body, once an obstacle, cooperates in Christian conduct" (p. 62).

9. Lettre de Pascal et de sa soeur Jacqueline à Mme Périer (1 April 1648), in *Oeuvres complètes*, ed. Louis Lafuma (Paris: Seuil, 1963), p. 273.

10. Ibid.

11. Ibid.

12. Many critics have argued that the three orders are discontinuous and operate in distinct domains, but Davidson (*Origins of Certainty*) convincingly argues that the three orders do in fact interrelate.

13. In *The Order of Things* (New York: Vintage, 1973), p. 57, Michel Foucault says that "the relation of all knowledge to the mathesis is posited as the possibility of establishing an ordered succession between things, even non-measurable ones. . . . This relation to *Order* is as essential to the Classical age as the relation to *Interpretation* was to the Renaissance."

14. René Descartes, *Discourse on Method*, trans. F. E. Sutcliffe (New York: Penguin, 1968), p. 41.

15. Ibid.

16. Blaise Pascal, "De l'Esprit géometrique," in *Oeuvres complètes*, ed. Louis Lafuma (Paris: Seuil, 1963), p. 349.

17. Ibid., p. 350.

18. Ibid.

19. Ibid.

20. Ibid.

21. The notion of humans as machines had become a commonplace in the seventeenth century, a notion much inspired by Cartesian thought. The famous Cartesian soul/body duality roughly corresponds to the distinction between the higher "human" quality of humankind, on the one hand, and its lower part, the animal-machine, on the other. Although Descartes recognized the importance of a mechanistic explanation for human thought and conduct, he sought to limit its explanatory powers. Other seventeenth-century writers, such as La Bruyère, sought, however, to extend and broaden the notion of the machinelike nature of humans. See Jules Brody, *Du Style à la pensée: Trois études sur les Caractères de La Bruyère* (Lexington: French Forum Publishers, 1980). For a more general discussion see Leonora C. Rosenfield, *From Beast-Machine to Man-Machine: The Theme of Animal Soul in French Letters from Descartes to La Mettrie* (New York: Octagon, 1968).

22. Philippe Sellier, in his edition of the *Pensées* (Paris: Mercure de France, 1976), recognizing the particular importance of the discourse of the machine, entitled the unclassified section on the wager, "The discourse of the machine."

23. This analysis is taken from my article, "Conventions of Meaning in Pascal's *Pensées*," *Papers on French Seventeenth Century Literature* 14 (1981): 71–84.

24. See Alfred Glauser, "Montaigne et le 'roseau pensant' de Pascal," *Romanic Review* 66 (1975):263–268.

25. Tzvetan Todorov, *Littérature et Signification* (Paris: Larousse, 1967), p. 102: "de nous faire prendre conscience de l'existence du discours, . . . de décrire l'aspect perceptible du discours humain."

26. Jean-Jacques Demorest, *Pascal Ecrivain: Etude sur les variantes de ses écrits* (Paris: Minuit, 1957), p. 17.

27. Roman Jakobson, "Linguistics and Poetics," in *Style in Language,* ed. Thomas Sebeok (Cambridge: MIT Press, 1960), p. 367.

28. For a general discussion of this phenomenon, see Todorov, *Littérature et Signification*, pp. 98–120.


## 3: Two Stories of the Fall and Desire: Paradise/Paradigm Lost

1. It may seem surprising to think of the *Pensées* as a narrative because the Pascalian scholarly tradition tends to treat them as a philosophical or theological discourse of truth, which we often assume does not take the narrative form. Narrative is, nonetheless, a vital component of the *Pensées,* although their fragmentary and disorderly form helps to cloak their essential narrative quality. Narrative is the quintessential fallen discourse. By virtue of its temporality and fictionality, narrative underlines its distance from the truth of divine discourse which knows neither time nor fiction.

Narrative is a product of the Fall and the notion of the Fall implies a narrative. Both the Fall and narrative are structured by a change in events from one temporal frame to another. The Fall is created by a shift from an ideal state of communication with God *before* the central event of Original Sin to a debased state of exile from God *after* this key event. In God, by contrast, there can be no narrative, for the Supreme Being exists outside time. God has no narrative extension. Pascal clearly follows Saint Augustine, who writes: "For your word is not speech in which each part comes to an end when it has been spoken, giving place to the next. . . . In your Word all is uttered at one and the same time, yet eternally" (*Confessions* XI.7). In contrast with divine, nonnarrative discourse, a temporal schema underlies human discourse and the structure of the Fall, necessitating two chronological frames. The first frame presents a positive model of plenitude, which is lacking in the second. Similarly, narrative is characterized in terms of temporal frames. It requires, as Gerald Prince notes, "the representation of at least two real or fictive events or situations in a time sequence" (*Narratology: The Form and Functioning of Narrative* [The Hague: Mouton, 1982], p. 4).

Human desire also engenders narrative. Desire requires a shift in a temporal sequence to counterbalance the shift created by the Fall. Rather than moving from a state of fullness to one of lack, however, desire moves from a state of lack to an imagined state of plenitude.

2. For a discussion of paradox in general, see Eric Gans, *Essais d'esthétique paradoxale* (Paris: Gallimard, 1977), and Rosalie Colie, *Paradoxia Epidemica* (Princeton: Princeton University Press, 1966).

3. For a discussion of the paradoxical nature of Pascal's thought, see

Lucien Goldmann, *Le Dieu caché: Etude sur la vision tragique dans les Pensées de Pascal et dans le théâtre de Racine* (Paris: Gallimard, 1959).

4. For Derrida, "Différance" [is] the result of a lack of "an originary presence" which can be interpreted as God. Thus, there is no present; all things are "deferred." According to Derrida, "Différance" comes from the Latin verb *differe,* which has two meanings. The first one is "the action of putting off until later, to account for time and forces in an operation that implies an economic calculation, a detour, a time limit, a delay, a doubt, a representation—all concepts I would sum up in a word I have already used, a word that could be inscribed in this chain: temporization. To defer, in this sense, is to temporize, to have recourse, consciously or unconsciously, to the temporal and temporizing mediation of a detour suspending the accomplishment or the fulfillment of a desire or an intention, executing it in a mode that cancels as well as in one that tempers its effect" ("l'action de remettre à plus tard, de tenir le compte du temps et des forces dans une opération qui implique un calcul économique, un détour, un délai, un retard, une réserve, une représentation, tous concepts que je résumerai ici d'un mot dont je ne me suis servi mais qu'on pourrait inscrire dans cette chaine: temporisation. Différer en ce sens, c'est temporiser, c'est recourir, consciemment ou inconsciemment, à la médiation temporelle et temporatrice d'un détour suspendant l'accomplissement ou le remplissement d'un 'désir' ou de la 'volonté' l'effectuant aussi bien sur un mode qui en annule ou en tempère l'effet" (Jacques Derrida, "La Différance," in *Tel Quel: Théorie d'ensemble* [Paris: Seuil, 1968], p. 46).

5. See Domna Stanton, "The Ideal of *Repos* in Seventeenth-Century French Literature," *L'Esprit créateur* 15 (1975):79–104. See also Etienne Gilson, *The Christian Philosophy of Saint Augustine* (New York: Random House, 1960).

6. Michel Foucault, *The Order of Things* (New York: Vintage, 1973), p. 27.

7. For the impact of the shift in paradigms, see Thomas Kuhn, *The Structure of Scientific Revolution* (Chicago: University of Chicago Press, 1972).

8. Ernst Cassirer, *The Individual and the Cosmos in Renaissance Philosophy,* trans. Mario Domandi (New York: Barnes and Noble, 1963), p. 175.

9. Ibid., p. 110.

10. See David Wetsel, *L'Ecriture et le reste: The Pensées of Pascal in the Exegetical Tradition of Port-Royal* (Columbus: Ohio State University Press, 1981).

11. Descartes, *Discourse on Method,* p. 78.

12. Francis Bacon, *The New Organon* (New York: Bobbs-Merrill, 1960), p. 78.

13. Ibid., p. 71.

14. See Basil Willey, *The Seventeenth Century Background: Studies in the*

*Thought of the Age in Relation to Poetry and Religion* (New York: Columbia University Press, 1958).

15. Sylvie Romanowski, *L'Illusion chez Descartes: La structure du discours cartésien* (Paris: Klincksieck, 1974), p. 11.

16. For Bruno, the infinite attests to the glory and greatness of God: "Thus is the excellence of God magnified and the greatness of his kingdom made manifest; he is glorified not in one, but in countless suns, not in a single earth, but in a thousand, I say, in an infinity of worlds" (*De l'Infinito universo e mondi*, cited in Alexander Koyré, *From the Closed World to the Infinite Universe* [Baltimore: Johns Hopkins University Press, 1968], p. 42).

17. See Romanowski, *L'Illusion chez Descartes*.

18. See Koyré, *From the Closed World*.

19. Ibid., p. 61.

20. Quoted in ibid., p. 189.

21. Friedrich Nietzsche, *The Gay Science*, trans. Walter Kaufmann, in *The Portable Nietzsche* (New York: Viking Press, 1954), pp. 95–96 (italics in original).

22. Friedrich Nietzsche, *The Will to Power*, trans. Walter Kaufmann, in *The Portable Nietzsche* (New York: Viking Press, 1954), p. 105.

23. Hans Jonas, *The Phenomenon of Life: Toward a Philosophical Biology* (New York: Delta, 1966), pp. 211–234. See also Karl Löwith, *Nature, History and Existentialism* (Evanston: Northwestern University Press, 1966).

24. Given the silence of the transcendent world, Sartre, in "Existentialism is a Humanism," argues that since "there are no signs in the world," man, "abandoned" and left to himself, reclaims his freedom or, rather, cannot help taking it upon himself: he "is" that freedom, man being "nothing but his own project," and "all is permitted to him."

25. For a detailed discussion of the Pascalian subject of discourse, see Louis Marin, *La Critique du discours* (Paris: Minuit, 1975), and "'Pascal': Text, Author, Discourse . . . ," *Yale French Studies* 52 (1975):129–151.

26. Paul Valéry, "Variation," in *Oeuvres complètes* (Paris: Pléiade, 1957), I:458–473.

27. André Gide, *La Porte étroite* (Paris: Folio, 1959), p. 139.

28. Henri Lefebvre, *Pascal* (Paris: Nagel, 1949), p. 2.

29. Albert Béguin, *Pascal par lui-même* (Paris: Seuil, 1952), pp. 45–46.

## 4: Reading in/of the *Pensées*

1. For a discussion of the opposition between the "optimistic rationalists" and the "pessimistic Augustinians" in seventeenth-century Christian apologetics, see Patricia Topliss, *The Rhetoric of Pascal: A Study of His*

*Art of Persuasion in the Provinciales and the Pensées* (Leicester: Leicester University Press, 1966).

2. In this regard, Augustine aligns himself with the tradition of negative theology.

3. See W. K. Flemming, *Mysticism in Christianity* (London: Robert Scott, 1913).

4. I owe this insight to my colleague James H. Reid, who is currently working on the problem of memory and forgetting in the modern French novel.

5. See Michel Foucault, *Les Mots et les choses* (Paris: Gallimard, 1966).

6. This fragment is not cited in either the Lafuma or the Sellier edition.

7. As a result, the notion of the reader cannot be universalized. I realize that my use of the pronoun "we" as a stylistic device fights against my argument by universalizing the notion of the reader. This pronoun is so embedded in the structure of the language, however, that I found it impossible to avoid it if I wanted to adhere to the conventions of clarity.

8. For a discussion of this metaphor, see Georges Poulet, *Les Métamorphoses du cercle* (Paris: Plon, 1949). Poulet notes that the metaphor was traditionally used to discuss God, but Pascal changes its signified to the infinite.

9. "De l'Art de persuader," *Oeuvres complètes*, ed. Lafuma (Paris: Intégrale, 1963), p. 358.

10. Louis Marin also raises the question of the subject in its discourse. He focuses on the proper name "Pascal" and on its pseudonym in the *Provinciales*, Louis de Montalte, whose anagram, Salomon de Tultie, appears in the *Pensées*. For Marin, the author's proper name, anagrammatically transformed into a pseudonym, is "the rhetorical *figure* of a manner of writing—a manner devoid of the Self since it is that of Grace, a manner 'revealed' and concealed by the anagram" (see "'Pascal': Text, Author, Discourse . . . ," *Yale French Studies* 52 [1975]:129). I am interested in the relationship between the "author" and previous texts.

11. "De l'Art de persuader," p. 357.

12. Ibid., p. 358.

13. See Bernard Croquette, *Pascal et Montaigne* (Geneva: Droz, 1974). Croquette places the Pascalian text next to its borrowed Montaignian portion to bring out the exact nature of the borrowings.

14. *Préface de l'Edition de Port-Royal* (1670), in *Oeuvres complètes* (Paris: Intégrale, 1963), p. 498.

15. Ibid.

16. Most efforts to reconstruct the plan relied either on internal evidence suggested by the fragments themselves or on external evidence or on both. The external evidence is offered by Fileau de la Chaise's *Discours sur les Pensées*, by Etienne Périer's *Préface de l'Edition de Port-Royal* (1670),

and by a study of Pascal's life, Christian apologetics, and the religious climate of the time.

17. For this blitzkrieg summary of editions, I have relied on Topliss, *Rhetoric of Pascal*, p. 156.

18. My discussion of the editions jumps from the 1880s to Lafuma, omitting the important editions of Michaut, Brunschvicg, Stewart, Chevalier, and others, because my goal is not to give a comprehensive history but merely to sketch out the general lines of the pursuit of an "objective text." For a more detailed discussion, see Anthony Pugh, *The Composition of Pascal's Apologia* (Toronto: University of Toronto Press, 1984).

19. The ultimate status of the partial classification of the *Pensées* into *liasses* is problematic. Lafuma took great pains to prove that this classification in the copy is actually that of Pascal himself. From this, both Lafuma and Jean Mesnard conclude that the copy was really the outline for the Pascalian text. Even if it were proven, however, that the order of the liasses is truly Pascal's order, one could argue that the copy did not necessarily provide the actual plan for the text. It is widely assumed that the classification was undertaken partly in preparation for Pascal's talk at Port-Royal. Although Pascal may have deemed it proper to present his material in one order for a particular audience (Port-Royal), he might have decided to change it to suit a different audience. It is also possible that the first order was merely provisional. As Pascal indicated it would take him ten years of good health to complete his project, he needed some order to give structure temporarily to his ideas: "The last thing one discovers in composing a work is what to put first" ("La dernière chose qu'on trouve en faisant un ouvrage, est de savoir celle qu'il faut mettre la première" [S740, L976, B19]). If the final order is one of the last things to be discovered, how could we expect Pascal to have already found it when he was just beginning his project? It seems likely that even Pascal did not yet know the order of his plan. The copy may simply represent a temporary organization to be revised at a later date. Moreover, Lafuma tends to overemphasize the fixity of this plan. It should be remembered that more than half of the fragments remained unclassified and that within each liasse the fragments are unordered. It was Lafuma as editor who devised an internal order for each liasse.

20. Two copies of the *Recueil Original* were made: the first is MS 9203 and the second is MS 12449. According to Philippe Sellier, the first copy was ruined by corrections made by Arnauld, Nicole, and Etienne Périer. The corrections were made in such a way that it is difficult to distinguish Pascal's original writing from the additions and changes made by these editors. The second copy, however, remains a more faithful rendition of Pascal's original thoughts and formulations. The only changes made

were in the transcription of the original. Thus, the second copy has remained essentially intact, whereas the first copy has been mutilated by various editors.

21. Lucien Goldmann, *Le Dieu caché: Etude sur la vision tragique dans les Pensées de Pascal et dans le théâtre de Racine* (Paris: Gallimard, 1959), p. 220.

22. Marin, "'Pascal': Text, Author," pp. 133–134.

23. Philippe Sellier, "Rhétorique et Apologie: 'Dieu parle bien de Dieu,'" in *Méthodes chez Pascal* (Paris: PUF, 1979); Domna Stanton, "Pascal's Fragmentary Thoughts: Dis-order and Its Overdetermination," *Semiotica* 51 (1984):211–235.

24. Stanton, "Pascal's Fragmentary Thoughts," p. 224.

25. Ibid., p. 226.

26. Ibid., p. 227.

27. Pascal, *Ecrits sur la Grâce*, in *Oeuvres complètes*, ed. Lafuma (Paris: Intégrale, 1963), p. 311.

28. Ibid.

# Bibliography

## I. EDITIONS OF PASCAL

*Complete Editions*

*Oeuvres de Blaise Pascal. Publiées suivant l'ordre chronologique, avec documents complémentaires, introductions et notes, par Léon Brunschvicg, Pierre Boutroux et Félix Gazier.* Paris: Hachette, 1908–1921. 14 vols.

*Oeuvres complètes.* Ed. Jacques Chevalier. Paris: Pléiade, 1936.

*Oeuvres complètes.* Ed. Louis Lafuma. Paris: Seuil, 1963.

*Pensées*

*Pensées de M. Pascal sur la religion, et sur quelques autres sujets, qui ont été trouvées après sa mort parmi ses papiers.* Edition de Port-Royal. Paris, 1670.

*Pensées de Pascal. Nouvelle édition corrigée et augmentée.* Ed. Condorcet. London, 1776.

*Eloge et Pensées de Pascal. Nouvelle édition, commentée, corrigée et augmentée par M. de \*\*\*.* Ed. Voltaire. Paris, 1778.

*Pensées, Fragments et Lettres de Blaise Pascal, publiés pour la première fois conformément aux manuscrits originaux, en grande partie inédits, par M. Prosper Faugère.* Paris: Andrieux, 1844. 2 vols.

*Pensées de Pascal, publiées dans leur texte authentique avec un commentaire suivi et une étude littéraire par Ernest Havet.* Paris: Dezobry and Magdeleine, 1852.

*Pensées de Pascal disposées suivant un plan nouveau par J. F. Astié.* Paris, 1857. 2 vols.

*Pensées de Pascal, publiées dans leur texte authentique et d'après le plan de l'auteur, avec une introduction et des notes, par J.-B. Jeannin.* Paris, 1883.

*Les Pensées de Pascal disposées suivant l'ordre du cahier autographe par G. Michaut.* Fribourg: Apud Bibliopolam Universitatis, 1896.

*Pensées et Opuscules publiés par Léon Brunschvicg.* Paris: Hachette, 1897.

*Pensées et Opuscules.* Ed. Léon Brunschvicg. Paris: Hachette, 1949.

*Original des Pensées. Fac-Simile du manuscrit 9202 (fonds français) de la Bibliothèque Nationale par Léon Brunschvicg.* Paris, 1905.

163

*Pascal. Pensées sur la vérité de la religion chrétienne par Jacques Chevalier.* Paris: Gabalda, 1925. 2 vols.

*Pensées. Edition critique établie par Zacharie Tourneur.* Paris: Cluny, 1938. 2 vols.

*Pensées de Blaise Pascal. Edition paléographique des manuscrits originaux présentée dans le classement primitif par Zacharie Tourneur.* Paris: Vrin, 1942.

*Le Manuscrit des Pensées de Pascal. Les feuillets autographes reclassés dans l'ordre de la Copie des Pensées. Edition introduite, annotée et établie par Louis Lafuma.* Paris: Les Libraires Associées, 1962.

*Pensées.* Ed. Louis Lafuma. Paris: Intégrale, 1963.

*Pensées.* Ed. Léon Brunschvicg. Paris: Hachette, 1964.

*Pensées: Nouvelle édition établie pour la première fois d'après la copie de référence de Gilberte Pascal.* Ed. Philippe Sellier. Paris: Mercure de France, 1976.

*Pensées.* Ed. Michel Le Guern. Paris: Folio, 1977. 2 vols.

*English Translations of Pensées*

*Pascal's Pensées.* Intro. by T. S. Eliot. New York: Dutton, 1958.

*The Pensées.* Trans. J. M. Cohen. Harmondsworth: Penguin, 1961.

*Pensées.* Trans. A. J. Krailsheimer. Harmondsworth: Penguin, 1966.

## II.  OTHER PRIMARY SOURCES

Aristotle. *The Poetics.* New York: Hill and Wang, 1961.

————. *The Rhetoric.* Harmondsworth: Penguin, 1965.

Arnauld, Antoine, and Nicole, Pierre. *La Logique ou l'art de penser.* Paris: Flammarion, 1970.

Augustine. *On Christian Doctrine.* Trans. D. W. Robertson, Jr. New York: Liberal Arts Press, 1958.

————. *Confessions.* Harmondsworth: Penguin, 1961.

Bacon, Francis. *The New Organon.* New York: Bobbs-Merrill, 1960.

Bary, R. *La Rhétorique française.* Paris, 1653.

Bouhours, D. *Les Entretiens d'Ariste et d'Eugène.* Paris: Cluny, 1962.

————. *La Manière de bien penser dans les ouvrages d'esprit.* Paris, 1688.

Descartes, René. *Oeuvres complètes.* Paris: Pléiade, 1937.

————. *Discours de la méthode.* Paris: Vrin, 1966.

————. *Discourse on Method.* Trans. F. E. Sutcliffe. New York: Penguin, 1968.

Gide, André. *La Porte étroite.* Paris: Folio, 1959.

Lamy, B. *La Rhétorique ou l'art de parler.* Paris, 1688.

Maimonides, Moses. *The Guide of the Perplexed.* Trans. Chaim Rabin. London: East-West Library, 1952.

Montaigne, Michel de. *Essais*. Ed. Maurice Rat. Paris: Pléiade, 1962.

Nietzsche, Friedrich. *The Complete Works*. Trans. Oscar Levy. New York: Macmillan, 1909–1911. 18 vols.

———. *Gesammelte Werke*. Munich: Musarion Verlag, 1922–1929. 23 vols.

———. *The Gay Science*. Trans. Walter Kaufmann. New York: Viking, 1954.

Périer, Etienne. "Préface de l'Edition de Port-Royal" (1670). In Pascal's *Oeuvres complètes*. Paris: Intégrale, 1963.

Plato. *The Phaedrus*. Ed. R. S. Bluck. Cambridge: Cambridge University Press, 1961.

———. *The Republic*. Trans. Allan Bloom. New York: Basic Books, 1968.

———. *The Meno*. Trans. W. K. C. Guthrie. New York: Bobbs-Merrill, 1971.

———. *The Gorgias*. Ed. W. H. Thompson. New York: Arno Press, 1973.

Sartre, Jean-Paul. "L'Existentialisme est un humanisme." Paris: Coll. Bibl. des idées, 1946.

Sénault, J. F. *L'Homme criminel*. 4th ed. Paris, 1656.

Valéry, Paul. "Variation." In *Oeuvres complètes*. Ed. Jean Hytier. Paris: Pléiade, 1957. Vol. 1.

Vaugelas, C. F. de. *Remarques sur la langue française utiles à ceux qui veulent bien parler et bien écrire*. Paris: Baudry, 1880.

## III. CRITICAL WORKS

Angers, Julien-Eymard d'. *L'Apologétique en France de 1550 à 1670: Pascal et ses précurseurs*. Paris: Nouvelles Editions Latines, 1954.

Baird, A. W. S. *Studies in Pascal's Ethics*. The Hague: Martinus Nijhoff, 1975.

Barth, Karl. *Church Dogmatics*. Edinburgh: T & T Clark, 1975.

Barthes, Roland. "L'Ancienne Rhétorique," *Communications* 16 (1970): 172–229.

Béguin, Albert. *Pascal par lui-même*. Paris: Seuil, 1952.

Bénichou, Paul. *Les Morales du grand siècle*. Paris: Gallimard, 1958.

Blanchot, M. *L'Entretien infini*. Paris: Gallimard, 1969.

Bloomberg, E. *Les Raisons de Pascal*. Paris: Debresse, 1973.

Bonhoeffer, Dietrich. *Ethics*. New York: Macmillan, 1955.

———. *Creation and Temptation*. London: SCM Press, 1966.

Borgerhoff, E. B. O. *The Freedom of French Classicism*. Princeton: Princeton University Press, 1950.

Bray, René. *La Formation de la doctrine classique en France*. Paris: Nizet, 1951.

Bremond, Henri. *Histoire littéraire du sentiment religieux*. Paris, 1938. 7 vols.

Brody, Baruch. *Readings in the Philosophy of Religion: An Analytic Approach.* Englewood Cliffs: Prentice-Hall, 1974.

Brody, Jules. *Boileau and Longinus.* Geneva: Droz, 1958.

————. *Du Style à la pensée: Trois études sur les Caractères de La Bruyère.* Lexington: French Forum Publishers, 1980.

Brody, Jules, ed. *French Classicism: A Critical Miscellany.* Englewood Cliffs: Prentice-Hall, 1966.

Broome, J. H. *Pascal: A Study of His Thought.* London: Arnold, 1975.

Brunschvicg, Léon. *Descartes et Pascal: lecteurs de Montaigne.* Paris: Plon, 1932.

Cassirer, Ernst. *The Individual and the Cosmos in Renaissance Philosophy.* Trans. Mario Domandi. New York: Barnes and Noble, 1963.

Chambers, Ross. *Meaning and Meaningfulness: Studies in the Analysis and Interpretation of Texts.* Lexington: French Forum Publishers, 1979.

Chatman, Seymour. *Story and Discourse.* Ithaca: Cornell University Press, 1978.

Chinard, G. *En lisant Pascal.* Geneva: Droz, 1948.

Chomsky, Noam. *Cartesian Linguistics: A Chapter in the History of Rationalist Thought.* New York: Harper and Row, 1966.

————. *Language and Mind.* New York: Harcourt Brace Jovanovich, 1972.

Colie, Rosalie. *Paradoxia Epidemica.* Princeton: Princeton University Press, 1966.

Croquette, Bernard. *Pascal et Montaigne.* Geneva: Droz, 1974.

Curtius, Ernst Robert. *European Literature in the Latin Middle Ages.* Trans. Willard Trask. Princeton: Princeton University Press, 1973.

Davidson, H. M., and Dubé, P. H. *A Concordance to Pascal's Pensées.* Ithaca: Cornell University Press, 1975.

Davidson, Hugh. *Audience, Words, and Art: Studies in Seventeenth-Century French Rhetoric.* Columbus: Ohio State University Press, 1965.

————. *The Origins of Certainty: Means and Meaning in Pascal's Pensées.* Chicago: University of Chicago Press, 1979.

De Man, Paul. *Allegories of Reading.* New Haven: Yale University Press, 1979.

Demorest, Jean-Jacques. *Dans Pascal: Essai en partant de son style.* Paris: Minuit, 1953.

————. *Pascal Ecrivain: Etude sur les variantes de ses écrits.* Paris: Minuit, 1957.

————. "Pascal's Sophistry and the Sin of Poesy." In *Studies in Seventeenth-Century Literature Presented to Morris Bishop.* Ed. J.-J. Demorest. Ithaca: Cornell University Press, 1962. Pp. 132–152.

Derrida, Jacques. *De la grammatologie.* Paris: Minuit, 1967.

————. *L'Ecriture et la différence.* Paris: Seuil, 1967.

――. "La Différance." In *Tel Quel: Théorie d'ensemble.* Paris: Seuil, 1968.

――. "Structure, Sign and Play." In *Structuralist Controversy.* Ed. Richard Macksey and Eugenio Donato. Baltimore: Johns Hopkins University Press, 1970.

――. *La Dissémination.* Paris: Seuil, 1972.

――. *Marges.* Paris: Minuit, 1972.

――. *Of Grammatology.* Trans. Gayatri Chakravorty Spivak. Baltimore: Johns Hopkins University Press, 1976.

Desgrippes, G. *Etudes sur Pascal, de l'automatisme à la foi.* Paris: Tégui, 1955.

Dionne, James. *Pascal et Nietzsche: étude historique et comparée.* New York: Burt Franklin, 1965.

Eco, Umberto. *L'Oeuvre ouverte.* Paris: Seuil, 1965.

――. *A Theory of Semiotics.* Bloomington: Indiana University Press, 1976.

――. *The Role of the Reader.* Bloomington: Indiana University Press, 1979.

Ernest, Pol. *Approches pascaliennes.* Gembloux: J. Duculot, 1970.

Foucault, Michel. *Les Mots et les choses.* Paris: Gallimard, 1966.

――. *L'Archéologie du savoir.* Paris: Gallimard, 1969.

――. *The Order of Things.* New York: Vintage, 1973.

Flemming, W. K. *Mysticism in Christianity.* London: Robert Scott, 1913.

France, Peter. *Rhetoric and Truth in France.* Oxford: Clarendon Press, 1972.

Francis, R. *Les Pensées de Pascal en France de 1842 à 1942.* Paris: Nizet, 1959.

François, Carlos. *La Notion de l'absurde dans la littérature française du XVIIᵉ siècle.* Paris: Klincksieck, 1972.

Gadamer, Hans-Georg. *Philosophical Hermeneutics.* Trans. and ed. David E. Linge. Berkeley, Los Angeles, London: University of California Press, 1976.

Gandillac, M. "Pascal et le silence du monde." In *Blaise Pascal: l'homme et l'oeuvre.* Cahiers de Royaumont. Paris: Minuit, 1956.

Gans, Eric. *Essais d'esthétique paradoxale.* Paris: Gallimard, 1977.

――. *The Origin of Language: A Formal Theory of Representation.* Berkeley, Los Angeles, London: University of California Press, 1981.

Gilson, Etienne. *The Christian Philosophy of Saint Augustine.* New York: Random House, 1960.

Girard, René. *Mensonge romantique et vérité romanesque.* Paris: Grasset, 1961.

Glauser, Alfred. "Montaigne et le 'roseau pensant' de Pascal," *Romanic Review* 66 (1975):263–268.

Goldmann, Lucien. *Le Dieu caché: Etude sur la vision tragique dans les Pensées de Pascal et dans le théâtre de Racine.* Paris: Gallimard, 1959.

Goldmann, Lucien, ed. *Correspondance de Marin de Barcos.* Paris: PUF, 1956.

Gouhier, Henri. *La Pensée métaphysique de Descartes.* Paris: Vrin, 1962.

————. *Blaise Pascal: Commentaires.* Paris: Vrin, 1966.

Harrington, Thomas. *Vérité et Méthode dans les Pensées de Pascal.* Paris: Vrin, 1972.

Hay, Malcolm. *The Prejudices of Pascal.* London: Neville Spearman, 1962.

Hubert, Sister Marie Louise. *Pascal's Unfinished Apology: A Study of His Plan.* New Haven: Yale University Press, 1952.

Iser, Wolfgang. *The Implied Reader.* Baltimore: Johns Hopkins University Press, 1974.

Jakobson, Roman. "Linguistics and Poetics." In *Style in Language.* Ed. Thomas Sebeok. Cambridge: MIT Press, 1960.

————. *Essais de linguistique générale.* Paris: Minuit, 1966.

Jameson, Fredric. *The Prison-House of Language.* Princeton: Princeton University Press, 1972.

Jonas, Hans. *The Phenomenon of Life: Toward a Philosophic Biology.* New York: Delta, 1966.

Jungo, Dom. *Le Vocabulaire de Pascal.* Paris: D'Artrey, 1950.

Keohane, Nannerl. *Philosophy and the State in France.* Princeton: Princeton University Press, 1980.

Kermode, Frank. *The Sense of an Ending.* London: Oxford University Press, 1966.

Kibedi-Varga, A. *Rhétorique et Littérature.* Paris: Didier, 1970.

Klein, Jacob. *A Commentary on Plato's Meno.* Chapel Hill: University of North Carolina Press, 1965.

Koyré, Alexander. *Etudes galiléennes.* Paris: Hermann, 1966.

————. *Etudes d'histoire de la pensée scientifique.* Paris: PUF, 1966.

————. *From the Closed World to the Infinite Universe.* Baltimore: Johns Hopkins University Press, 1968.

Krailsheimer, A. J. *Pascal.* Oxford: Oxford University Press, 1980.

Kritzman, Lawrence, ed. *Fragments: Incompletion and Discontinuity.* New York: New York Literary Forum, 1981.

Kuentz, Pierre. "Le 'rhétorique' ou la mise à l'écart," *Communications* 16 (1970):143–157.

Kuhn, Thomas. *The Structure of Scientific Revolution.* Chicago: University of Chicago Press, 1972.

Lafuma, Louis. *Recherches pascaliennes.* Paris, 1949. 2 vols.

————. *Controverses pascaliennes.* Paris: Editions du Luxembourg, 1954.

————. *Histoire des Pensées de Pascal.* Paris: Editions du Luxembourg, 1954.

Langer, Susanne. *Philosophy in a New Key.* Cambridge: Harvard University Press, 1942.

Laporte, Jean. *La Doctrine de la Grâce chez Arnauld.* Paris: PUF, 1922.

————. *Le Coeur et la raison selon Pascal.* Paris: Elzévir, 1950.

Lefebvre, Henri. *Pascal.* Paris: Nagel, 1949.

Le Guern, Michel. *L'Image dans l'oeuvre de Pascal.* Paris: Colin, 1969.
———. *Pascal et Descartes.* Paris: Nizet, 1971.
Lewis, Philip. *La Rochefoucauld: The Art of Obstruction.* Ithaca: Cornell University Press, 1977.
Lhermet, J. *Pascal et la Bible.* Paris, 1949.
Lohmann, Elise. *Pascal und Nietzsche.* Leipzig: Druck von Robert Naske, 1917.
Lossky, Vladimir. *Théologie négative et connaissance de Dieu chez Maître Eckhart.* Paris: Vrin, 1960.
Lowith, Karl. *Nature, History and Existentialism.* Evanston: Northwestern University Press, 1966.
Macksey, Richard, and Donato, Eugenio, eds. *The Structuralist Controversy.* Baltimore: Johns Hopkins University Press, 1970.
Maggioni, Sister Mary Louise. *The Pensées of Pascal: A Study in Baroque Style.* Washington: Catholic University Press, 1950.
Magnard, P. *Nature et histoire dans l'Apologétique de Pascal.* Paris: Les Belles Lettres, 1975.
Marin, Louis. "Réflexions sur la notion de modèle chez Pascal," *Revue de Métaphysique et de Morale* 72 (1965):89–108.
———. *Etudes sémiologiques, Ecritures, Peintures.* Paris: Klincksieck, 1971.
———. *La Critique du discours.* Paris: Minuit, 1975.
———. "'Pascal': Text, Author, Discourse . . . ," *Yale French Studies* 52 (1975):129–151.
———. "On the Interpretation of Ordinary Language: A Parable of Pascal." In *Textual Strategies: Perspectives in Post-Structuralist Criticism.* Ed. Josué V. Harari. Ithaca: Cornell University Press, 1979.
Melzer, Sara E. "Codes of Space in the *Pensées,*" *French Review* 51 (1978): 816–824.
———. "Conventions of Meaning in Pascal's *Pensées,*" *Papers on French Seventeenth Century Literature* 14 (1981):71–84.
———. "*Invraisemblance* in Pascal's *Pensées:* The Anti-Rhetoric," *Romantic Review* 73 (1982):33–44.
———. "Pascal's *Pensées:* Economy and the Interpretation of Fragments," *Stanford French Review* 6 (1982):207–220.
Mesnard, Jean. "La Théorie des figuratifs dans les *Pensées* de Pascal," *Revue d'histoire de la philosophie* 35 (1943):219–253.
———. *Pascal: L'Homme et l'oeuvre.* Paris: Connaissance des Lettres, 1951.
———. *Les Pensées de Pascal.* Paris: SEDES, 1976.
Miel, Jan. "Pascal, Port-Royal and Cartesian Linguistics," *Journal of the History of Ideas* 30 (1969):230–245.
———. *Pascal and Theology.* Baltimore: Johns Hopkins University Press, 1969.

Morot-Sir, Edouard. *La Métaphysique de Pascal.* Paris: PUF, 1973.

————. *Pascal.* Paris: PUF, 1973.

————. "Du nouveau sur Pascal?" *Romance Notes* 18 (1977):272–279.

Natoli, Charles. *Nietzsche and Pascal on Christianity.* New York: Peter Lang, 1985.

Nelson, Robert. *Pascal: Adversary and Advocate.* Cambridge: Harvard University Press, 1981.

Norman, Buford. "Thought and Language in Pascal," *Yale French Studies* 49 (1973):110–119.

————. "Logic and Anti-Rhetoric in Pascal's *Pensées,*" *French Forum* 2 (1977):22–33.

Ong, Walter J. *Ramus: Method and the Decay of Dialog.* Cambridge: Harvard University Press, 1958.

Otto, Rudolf. *The Idea of the Holy: An Inquiry into the Non-Rational Factor in the Idea of the Divine and Its Relation to the Rational.* London: Oxford University Press, 1957.

Poulet, Georges. *Les Métamorphoses du cercle.* Paris: Plon, 1949.

Prince, Gerald. *A Grammar of Stories.* The Hague: Mouton, 1973.

————. "Introduction à l'étude du narrataire." *Poétique* 14 (1973):178–196.

————. *Narratology: The Form and Functioning of Narrative.* The Hague: Mouton, 1982.

Pugh, Anthony. *The Composition of Pascal's Apologia.* Toronto: University of Toronto Press, 1984.

Ramsey, Ian. *Words about God.* London: SCM Press, 1971.

Reiss, Timothy J. "The Word/World Equation," *Yale French Studies* 49 (1973):3–12.

————. "Cartesian Discourse and Classical Ideology," *Diacritics* (1976): 19–27.

————. "The 'Concevoir' Motif in Descartes." In *La Cohérence Intérieure: études sur la littérature française du XVII<sup></sup> siècle.* Paris: J. M. Place, 1977. Pp. 203–222.

————. "Sailing to Byzantium: Classical Discourse and its Self-Absorption," *Diacritics* (1978):34–46.

————. *The Discourse of Modernism.* Ithaca: Cornell University Press, 1982.

Ricoeur, Paul. *Finitude et culpabilité.* Paris: Aubier, 1960.

————. *Le Conflit des interprétations.* Paris: Seuil, 1969.

————. *La Métaphore vive.* Paris: Seuil, 1975.

Riffaterre, Michael. *La Production du texte.* Paris: Seuil, 1979.

Rodis-Lewis, Geneviève. *Descartes: Initiation à sa philosophie.* Paris: Vrin, 1974.

Romanowski, Sylvie. *L'Illusion chez Descartes: La structure du discours cartésien.* Paris: Klincksieck, 1974.

Rosenfield, Leonora C. *From Beast-Machine to Man-Machine: The Theme of Animal Soul in French Letters from Descartes to La Mettrie.* New York: Octagon, 1968.

Ross, James. "Analogy and the Resolution of Some Cognitivity Problems," *Journal of Philosophy* 67 (1970):725–746.

Rousset, Jean. *L'Intérieur et l'extérieur.* Paris: Corti, 1968.

Russier, Jean. *La Foi selon Pascal.* Paris: PUF, 1949. 2 vols.

Sebeok, Thomas. *Style in Language.* Cambridge: MIT Press, 1960.

Sellier, Philippe. *Pascal et la liturgie.* Paris: PUF, 1966.

———. *Pascal et Saint Augustin.* Paris: Colin, 1970.

———. "Rhétorique et Apologie: 'Dieu parle bien de Dieu.'" In *Méthodes chez Pascal.* Paris: PUF, 1979.

Stanton, Domna. "The Ideal of *Repos* in Seventeenth-Century French Literature," *Esprit créateur* 15 (1975):79–104.

———. "Playing with Signs: The Discourse of Molière's Dom Juan," *French Forum* 5 (1980):106–121.

———. "Pascal's Fragmentary Thoughts: Dis-order and Its Overdetermination," *Semiotica* 51 (1984):211–235.

Strowski, F. *Pascal et son temps.* Paris: Plon, 1907–1908. 2 vols.

Suleiman, Susan, and Crossman, Inge, eds. *The Reader in the Text.* Princeton: Princeton University Press, 1980.

Todorov, Tzvetan. *Littérature et signification.* Paris: Larousse, 1967.

Topliss, Patricia. *The Rhetoric of Pascal: A Study of His Art of Persuasion in the Provinciales and the Pensées.* Leicester: Leicester University Press, 1966.

Tourneur, Z. *Beauté poétique.* Melun: Rozelle, 1933.

Vamos, Maria. "Pascal's *Pensées* and the Enlightenment," *Studies in Voltaire and the Eighteenth Century* 97 (1972):1–145.

Wetsel, David. *L'Ecriture et le reste: The Pensées of Pascal in the Exegetical Tradition of Port-Royal.* Columbus: Ohio State University Press, 1981.

Willey, Basil. *The Seventeenth Century Background: Studies in the Thought of the Age in Relation to Poetry and Religion.* New York: Columbia University Press, 1958.

Wolfson, Harry. *Studies in the History of Philosophy and Religion.* Cambridge: Harvard University Press, 1973.

Woshinsky, Barbara. "Biblical Discourse: Reading the Unreadable," *Esprit créateur* 21 (1981):13–24.

Designer:      U.C. Press Staff
Compositor:    Janet Sheila Brown
Printer:       Edwards Brothers, Inc.
Binder:        Edwards Brothers, Inc.
Text:          Baskerville 10/12
Display:       Palatino